# GARDEN
# CONSTRUCTION
# IN PICTURES

# GARDEN CONSTRUCTION
## in pictures

**ADRIENNE
and
PETER OLDALE**

DRAKE PUBLISHERS INC : NEW YORK

ISBN 0-87749-357-X
LCCCN 73-10925

Published in 1974 by
Drake Publishers Inc
381 Park Avenue South
New York, N.Y. 10016

Printed in Great Britain

# CONTENTS

# INTRODUCTION

This book shows you how to construct a garden. Starting from the bare ground (or weed-covered patch!) it takes you step by step through clearing the weeds, digging the soil, and providing proper drainage. Next comes the layout of lawns with seed or turf; then the planting of shrubs, hedges and trees—all important jobs early on in the construction of any garden.

Laying out paths or patios in stone, brick or concrete, erecting walls, steps and rustic work, and making various items of furniture for use in the garden are all jobs that can be safely and easily done by amateurs. Simple structures in brick or stonework and many kinds of attractive wooden items can be made using only cheap and ordinary tools. Special skill is not required. The picture series show in close-up detail exactly how to go about the work.

Garden construction work does not call for the same accuracy as, for example, house building. It does not matter much if your stone wall wavers a little or if the flight of steps leading up to the rockery is not quite regular. In fact such irregularities may add to the charm of the garden. What is certain, though, is that all such structures must be safe and serviceable. They will be, if you follow the instructions carefully.

This book is meant first of all for the complete beginner, who may never before have used a spade, fork, or even a hammer and saw, but it also shows many jobs that can be tackled later, as skill develops.

Even if your garden is not new you may want to develop or alter it. The principles of work are exactly the same, and you will find most of the items equally suitable for the established garden.

Building or remodelling your own garden is not only a fascinating hobby but also saves all the cost of garden labour. The cost of materials is comparatively small. Nor need amateur work be unpleasing. Given care, time and patience you can do most things as well as the professional. The home worker can take his time, making up for possible lack of skill by extra painstaking care. All too often professional workers have to rush jobs to get them done at a reasonable cost. The amateur is under no such pressures. Some of the best gardens have been made by people with little practical professional experience.

# PLANNING SAVES TIME AND LABOUR

## PREPARING YOUR PROGRAMME

When laying out a new garden you can save much time and effort by planning the work carefully beforehand. Weeks of labour may be avoided by spending an hour with pencil and paper.

To begin with, much of the basic work in garden building lies in the cultivation of soil. But some parts of the garden, such as the lawn areas, do not really need *deep* digging. By marking these out beforehand you can save your main digging effort for shrub borders, rose beds and vegetable gardens, where there has to be deep cultivation. For the biggest plants of all, trees and large shrubs, it is still not always necessary to dig over the whole bed. Each one can be put into a deep planting-pit, roughly 4ft (120cm) in diameter.

Another advantage of careful pre-planning is that you then know the layout of your future paths and patios and can fit them into the programme of work. Obviously, the land where these run requires no cultivation at all. Foundations must be dug, and the valuable top soil can then be taken away to cover areas of poorer soil or to construct rockeries and raised beds. Into the foundation trenches go all the innumerable bricks and stones which infest most new gardens. These when broken and rammed will form ideal foundations for any kind of path.

Since all path foundations must be well consolidated you can use the roughly stoned 'paths' for the wheeling in of heavy materials such as lawn turves, slabs, blocks and so on. The more traffic these foundations carry, the more solidly the stones will be packed and the better the result when the path is eventually completed.

Some jobs in the garden are pretty heavy. One of these is the laying of lawns with turf. Newcomers often plan to lay out a large lawn in a weekend, perhaps not realising that turf for a lawn 10 × 10yd (m) weighs approximately 3 tons! All this weight must be carried from the roadside, placed on the ground and handled several times before the lawn is complete. But if such a job is planned for completion in stages, the preparation of the soil can be done over a period of months and the turves can be bought and laid in smaller units over a number of weeks throughout the autumn and early spring.

Another heavy job that calls for sensible planning is of course the actual laying of paths and patios. An area of patio 30 × 10ft (10 × 3m) or the equivalent area of pathway in, say, stone slabs would require approximately 4 tons of materials. Again all this normally has to be carted from the roadside, since delivery is usually made only to your front approach: but try asking for delivery to your rear gate – it could cut hours from a job. Concrete mixing and laying are also heavy items whilst even planting can be hard work when deeply dug tree planting-pits are needed.

Putting in of plants is mainly light and easy work. The weight is usually trifling and the job itself so interesting that it goes along well. However, it is a job that requires patience and, above all, *the right weather*. To avoid losses you must plan as far as possible to avoid both frosty periods or times of summer drought.

## STAGES IN CONSTRUCTING A NEW GARDEN

1. Clearing the soil. This means removing the weed cover which is almost inevitable on fresh land and can be anything from a light covering of annual weeds to a tangled mass of jungle. You may decide to kill the weeds with poisons, skim them away and burn them, dig them deeply underground to improve the soil, or fork them out for rotting into compost.

2. Dealing with drainage problems. It is much easier done at this stage than after the garden has been completed!

3. Cultivating the cleared ground. As described above, this is organised around the final plan of the garden. Shallow cultivation, as a rule, over lawns and similar areas; rather deeper work over flower beds; deeper still for shrubs, roses and where hedges are to run and, finally, planting pits for trees.

4. Excavating and making path foundations. The top soil is removed for use elsewhere. Stones and rubble are thrown in and consolidated by use for transport of turves and other heavy material.

5. Laying lawns, and in the neighbouring beds planting shrubs, hedges and trees.

6. Laying paths and patios. Do not tackle too much at once, and bear in mind that these are likely to be the most expensive items in your whole garden. A few yards of stone will almost certainly cost more than all the plants you put in!

7. Erecting fences or improving existing ones. Most new houses already have some sort of boundary screen, but this may be only a simple post and wire fence which could be transformed by installing panels or other wooden fencing.

Again, this is often best done in the early stages, if only because digging the post-holes and erecting the panels is bound to disturb any nearby flowers or shrubs.

8. Constructing walls. Here we are not likely to be working on a big scale. Indeed, for safety's sake, amateurs should never build walls (except perhaps, in lightweight screen-blocks) taller than about 3ft (1m). Remember how much you can save by casting your own slabs and blocks for paving and walls. It is easily done but not light work, so spread it over a few weekends before the slabs are needed.

9. The finishing touches. With the garden nearing completion you can begin to think about rustic decorative work, trellises and furniture. All these are easy to make, as are also cold frames and similar pieces of garden equipment.

# CLEARING THE GROUND

First, get rid of the weeds!

Spray with a poison such as sodium chlorate which will kill all plants (but the ground cannot afterwards be used for six months, until it has washed away) or paraquat which allows sowing and planting within a matter of days after application. Follow the manufacturer's directions exactly, and **store the poisons where children cannot possibly get at them, and in their original containers.**

To deal with really heavy growth you can hire a machine (*right*) to cut down tall vegetation.

Alternatively, in a small area you can skim off the weeds with a little of their soil (*centre right*) and cart them away to the compost heap. Burning the weeds is also possible but it is better to save them and rot them down. Many new gardens have poor soil which is best improved by composting all the plant material available.

## THE IMPORTANCE OF COMPOST

Compost is one of the most valuable of garden fertilisers. It is beneficial to all soils and is cheap and easy to make.

It is *not* enough simply to heap up soft green waste such as lawn mowings into an unpleasant, soggy pile. To make good compost you really need a compost container (*right*). This enables you to build deep piles, well aerated at the base and sides. Such a container can be knocked together out of timber and wire netting quite easily (see page 144).

Compost is made from domestic or garden waste, old wood, sawdust, animal manures and so on, which all gradually rot down into the black humus which most soils require. This can only take place when the heap is uniformly moist, with air circulating freely in all parts of it. To help it to rot evenly, each heap is turned every six weeks or so.

You can buy commercial activators which are sprinkled into the compost to start off the rotting process. These do work but are not essential, especially if you have available a little animal manure, which contains the bacteria necessary.

Compost is often slightly acid and a few handfuls of powdered lime scattered at intervals through the pile will greatly improve the final result. Some gardeners also use sulphate of ammonia to provide nitrogen on which the beneficial bacteria can live. This is not so essential in a well-mixed heap containing a wide range of garden refuse.

Keep the compost container in a sheltered place with good access from the side, so that the turning can be easily done.

Too much water spoils the compost, so lay a polythene sheet lightly over the heap to protect it from heavy rain.

The ideal garden would have several compost bins: one for fresh material; one or more for turned material and one for the compost actually ready for use. In this way a succession of good compost is assured throughout the year.

## MAKING GOOD COMPOST

(*a*) Good aeration is essential. Stand loose bricks around the base of the container spaced 1in (2.5cm) apart to allow the air access. Then lay down a first layer of very coarse material such as lengths of timber and tree prunings. This will rot down in due course, but meantime keeps the base of the heap airy and allows surplus water to drain away.

(*b*) Next place a 6in (15cm) layer of coarse material to support the higher layers of finer material.

(*c*) Garden waste of all kinds (grass rakings in the photograph) are spread evenly and well mixed to a depth of about 6in (15cm).

(*d*) An ideal compost container has one open side which can be gradually closed as the heap rises (see pages 144–5). Over the first layer of compost material scatter a 1in (2.5cm) covering of ordinary soil finely broken. Too much heavy soil may clog up the pile and spoil the air circulation. Never tread down, for the same reason.

(*e*) Bacteria to start off the rotting process are easily given in a forkful of well-rotted farmyard or horse manure. Alternatively, commercial activators can be used, as directed by the manufacturers.

(*f*) Ordinary domestic refuse of every kind except plastic, paper, metal and glass can go into the compost heap.

A sprinkling of hydrated lime over the alternate layers, mixed well in with the material as it is loaded, will reduce the acidity of the compost and help the rotting process.

After four to six weeks, depending on the conditions, the heap will be ready for its first turning. Remove the whole of the compost and replace, outside to middle.

The exact time compost takes to rot down completely to humus depends on climate, season and type of material.

Give the prepared compost a light covering against the clogging effect of heavy rain, but *not* an airtight sheet.

# DRAINAGE IN A SMALL GARDEN

Few plants grow well in waterlogged ground. Lawns especially need well-drained land.

The principles of draining are easy to understand. Pipes or stone-filled channels carry water away from the soil surface to a suitable outlet deeper in the ground. However, few town gardens have a water outlet into a ditch. Instead we must build a *soakaway*. This is simply a large hole into which the drains are led. It is *not* a pond (or once full it would be useless), but is dug deeply into a porous layer of subsoil from where water can find its own way deep into the ground.

The pit is not left open but is packed with coarse material such as stones, clinker, bricks and gravel which fill the hole without retaining water.

The drainage channels themselves may be anything from trenches filled with broken stone (or even thin branches of trees) to proper clay pipe drains. It is always best to lay pipes, though the expense may be considerable in a large garden.

## THE SOAKAWAY PIT

(*a*) First dig the soakaway pit, 3–4ft (1–1.5m) square, in the lowest convenient part of the land. Remove the top 10in (25cm) or so of fertile soil and set it carefully aside.

(*b*) Below this fertile soil you will find layer upon layer of subsoil of poorer quality and perhaps even a belt of clay. Dig this out and keep it separate from the top soil. The exact depth of the pit depends on the kind of ground. At the very least it must be 4ft (1.5m) deep and pass through any impervious layer of clay. Otherwise, it will merely act as a pond and not as a soakaway.

(*c*) Start to refill the pit using coarse broken stones, bricks or clinker.

f

g

## THE DRAINS

(d) The drains may run directly to the pit in small gardens. In large areas it is better to lay one main drain with 4in (10cm) diameter pipes running to the soakaway and join a number of branch drains of 3in (8cm) pipes to this. Space the smaller drains roughly 15ft (5m) apart. The slope of the trenches must be not less than about 1 in 20. So a 20ft (6m) drain will be at least 1ft (30cm) lower at the soakaway than at its outer end. The pipes must be at least 15in (38cm) deep at the shallowest end. Remember as before to keep the top soil separate from the coarser subsoil.

(e) Drain trenches must slope *evenly* or the water will not flow away properly. To check this use what are commonly called 'boning rods'. These are simply a set of three T-shaped wooden frames made from 2 × 1in (5 × 2.5cm) timber nailed together. It will be found convenient to have them 3ft (1m) tall and 1ft 6in (45cm) across the T-piece, unless your trenches are very deep. Stand them upright on the bottom of each trench, supporting them with bricks. Sight along their tops to check the trench slope.

(f) In short drains you can lay a straight board along the tops of the rods.

(g) Then to check whether the fall is of the right amount, rest one end of the board on the outermost boning rod and raise the other. Rest a spirit level on its upper edge. When the board is dead level measure the distance between its bottom and the top of the lowest boning rod. Divide this into the distance between these two rods to give you the exact 'fall'.

(h) Lay the pipes on a bed of fine soil or sand in the base of each trench. They should touch, but do not require fastening at the joints. Water finds its way into the pipes here. Where the pipe enters the soakaway protect it with larger stones and a tile to prevent the outlet becoming blocked by small pieces of stone, mud and dirt.

(i) Fill up beside the pipes with broken stones, carefully packed to prevent the pipes moving from side to side. It is good practice too to lay a piece of old tile over each joint.

(j) Then fill up the trenches with a coarse stone mixture, with finer gravel on top, to 10in (25cm) below the surface.

(k) The various pipes entering the soakaway are shown here just before the pit is almost filled in similar fashion.

Finally, cover the top of pit and drain channels with top soil. Slightly overfill to allow for settlement.

h

i

j

k

13

# CULTIVATION

## WHY DIG?

Some gardeners never dig their soil at all. They simply scatter over it large quantities of compost produced each year in several large heaps. This no-digging method is successful but few small gardens can make sufficient compost to keep the soil in good condition. Certainly in new gardens digging is the easiest way to improve the soil. It breaks up solid subsoil, improves drainage, allows air to enter the soil, and gives an opportunity for incorporating rich manures right down where the plant roots can find them. Lime also is often needed, the amount required being best decided by testing a thimbleful of soil with chemicals. Simple soil-testing sets are cheap and easy to use, needing no technical skill. They are a good investment.

Not all plants need the same *depth* of fertile soil. As we noted before, lawns, shrub borders, large shrubs and trees all require progressively deeper cultivation; soil preparation starts by marking out the areas required for each of these.

The photographs opposite show the simplest method of cultivation – *single digging*. This consists of turning over the top 8–10in (20–25cm) of soil, and working into it fertilisers and soil conditioners.

When working on most soils it is important, as a general rule, not to consolidate them. This is vital on really heavy kinds such as clay. So wherever possible do the work on such soils whilst standing on a broad plank. This prevents the ground from becoming compressed.

## SINGLE DIGGING

(*a*) Turn the soil over 8–10in (20–25cm) deep and chop down the largest lumps roughly with the spade.

(*b*) Granulated peat is one of the best of all soil improvers and good for both light and heavy soils. To sandy kinds it gives extra humus and water-retaining capacity; in clay, it helps to keep the particles apart, so improving soil texture and drainage. Always apply peat liberally. Spread it thickly over the surface. A dressing of general fertiliser can be given at the same time.

(*c*) Hoe the peat down into the top 2–3in (5–7.5cm) of the soil. Aim to produce a crumbly, free-draining texture. Another good conditioner for heavy land is coarse washed sand, spread thickly and worked shallowly into the soil.

(*d*) On medium or light land, and in dry conditions, a seed bed can be best produced by alternate treading of the ground underfoot . . .

(*e*) . . . and raking to give a fine yet firm-textured surface, ideal for most seeding and especially for lawns. Do *not* work this way on wet, heavy clay. This must be kept open, so tread it as little as possible.

a

b

c

d

e

# PREPARING FOR
# LAWNS—LEVELLING

To grow a successful lawn you must get the surface absolutely flat. A lumpy lawn is very difficult to maintain. Major irregularities are roughly levelled during the digging, but the final work is done with the rake.

Tackle this job by the method shown here, which can be adapted to any size of lawn.

(*a*) First rake the surface up into a fine tilth. Obviously, try to get the surface approximately level but do not spend much time on it at this stage.

(*b*) Next prepare several guide pegs roughly 15in (38cm) long and with their top ends marked off at 2in (5cm) intervals.

(*c*) Drive these pegs in, around and across the lawn, spacing them about 8ft (2.5m) part. You should have ready a long, straight board that can span the gap. Their exact position does not matter but the whole plot must be covered.

(*d*) Leave the marked section of the pegs protruding from the ground. Lay the board across the tops of a pair of pegs and place a spirit-level on it. Drive the pegs in as necessary until the board is perfectly level. Move on now from one of these pegs to a neighbouring peg, getting this one level and moving from it to the next, till the whole area has been covered. Some pegs may protrude high out of the ground

and others be even totally below ground level! The pegs now act as guides to raking. Continue until the soil is at the same marked level on every peg. It may be at the level of the top of each peg, the first mark, one second or any other. Provided that the soil is at the *same* mark on every peg, it will be level.

(*e*) Lay the board along the soil to make sure that it is flat *between* the pegs also. Where sloping lawns are to be flattened, use similar pegs, aligned with the 'boning rods' shown in our drainage section (page 12). Leave the pegs in place till after seeding or turf-laying is completed.

(*f*) A fine, evenly firm and crumbly soil is very important. For this, frequent re-raking is needed, with *light* rolling in between. Few newcomers to gardening own a roller, so a good plan is to make a pair of treading boards. These are simply 15in (38cm) lengths of planking 8in (20cm) or 10in (25cm) wide with two large loops of strong cord encircling them.

(*g*) Step firmly onto the boards and draw the loops taut to hold them to your feet.

(*h*) With a little practice you can walk on these boards and produce a flat, firm surface which after careful raking will give you a soil ready for a first-class lawn.

**See page 147: A useful raking and levelling tool.**

a

b

c

d

e

g

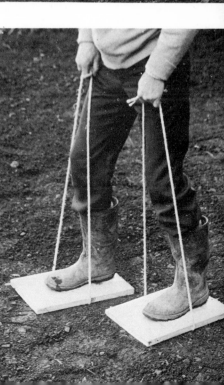

h

a

# MARKING OUT—A FEW TIPS

When you make a new garden or alter an old one you have to mark out the shapes of lawns, beds and paths, This is not usually very difficult but it is useful to know how to mark out easily and quickly a large right angle or perfectly square corner of 90°. You will need three wooden pegs and roughly 13yd (13m) of strong cord.

(a) Tie the cord to the pegs, spacing them 3yd (m), 4yd (m) and 5yd (m) apart (the extra yard/metre of rope is for the knots). Tie the cord ends to form a closed loop.

(b) Take the peg that comes between the 3yd and 4yd (m) sections and push it into the ground at the exact point where you want the corner.

(c) Draw out the 3yd (m) length along one side of the desired corner and push its end peg into the soil.

(d) Finally draw out the third peg as far as it will go. This will complete a triangle. The corner opposite the *longest* side is always a perfect right angle. Provided the proportions of the triangle are 3, 4 and 5, this corner is always exactly 90°.

(e) A circle is of course easy to mark out. Simply drive a peg into its centre and sweep another peg round at the end of a cord whose length is half the required diameter.

(f) However, these markings are easily lost during subsequent work. A sprinkling of ordinary flour will keep the outlines visible, and give a useful idea of the appearance of the desired paths, beds and lawns.

b

c ◀

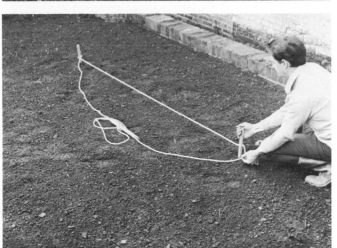

d ▶

e ◀

f ▶

# A LAWN WITH SEED

The best way to make a good-quality lawn is to sow seed. There are proprietary seed mixtures available to suit most requirements, whether these be for a fine lawn, or a hard-wearing or quick growing one. They are completely reliable. Prepare the soil well in advance so that it has time to settle. Any resulting weeds, humps and hollows can then be removed before the seed is actually sown. Surface drainage, in all but light soils, is improved by working *coarse* sand into the top 2–3in (5–7cm): no grass grows well in wet soil.

**a**

You can sow lawn seed in late summer or early spring. Avoid frost on grass seedlings, and, naturally, do not sow seed when the soil is completely parched. Try to choose a period of fine moist weather. A light dusting with bonemeal with the last raking just before seeding will be helpful.

Weeds may appear whilst the seed is germinating. Do not attempt to pull them out. Damage to the developing grass roots will more than outweigh any good done. In any case they will most be annuals and die after the first mowing.

Allow the grass to grow 2in (5cm) high, then mow it with a *sharp* mower set at 1½in (3.5cm). Over succeeding weeks gradually lower the blades to approximately ¾in (2cm). *Rolling* should not normally be required. It tends to consolidate the surface too strongly, especially on heavy soils.

Do not distribute strong fertilisers over newly-seeded lawns. If the weather turns dry after seeding the only solution is to keep sprinklers going *continually*. It is important *not* to start spraying unless you are able to keep it up for at least two weeks: the first few hours of watering cause the development of roots near the surface and if the watering is then stopped the subsequent drying out of the soil will shrivel these roots and may injure the grass irreparably.

**b**

## THIS WAY FOR BEST RESULTS

(*a*) Seed is usually sown at a rate of 2oz per square yard, distributed as evenly as possible. Mark the boundary of the lawn with strings; then lay a broad plank across the surface, exactly 1yd (1m) from one lawn-edge, and work from this.

(*b*) Measure enough seed into a bowl to cover the whole length of the yard-wide strip. (Try mixing the seed with twice its own volume of coarse sand to distribute evenly.)

(*c*) Seed should not be deeply buried. Rake it just below the surface with a very light rake.

(*d*) For best results sieve fine, moist peat over the newly-sown seed. This provides a moisture 'reservoir' and protects the seed from burning by hot sun.

**c**

**d**

With the first yard-strip seeded, move your treading board a yard across your plot and repeat the operation until the lawn is complete.

Protection from birds need not worry you: seed is usually pre-treated with a deterrent.

19

# LAYING A TURF LAWN

It is not difficult to lay a turf lawn. Good turf will soon settle down and grow. But there is a lot of labour in the job because of the weight of the turf: 100 square yards (metres) weigh roughly 3 tons, and all this must be carried into place, spread out and rammed by hand. Therefore do not try to lay too much in a single day. It is better to arrange for your turf to be delivered in three or four small lots rather than one large load.

Soil preparation is important but need not be carried to extremes. Turf brings with it a strong root system and a quantity of soil. It will grow even on plain raked gravel!

But a firm, flat surface is essential. It is difficult to correct hollows and humps after the turf has been put down.

The ideal seasons for turf laying are early spring or late autumn, but any moist period will do. Avoid summer as dry weather will cause the turves to shrink. Gaps so caused can be repaired by filling them with plain soil but the result is a weakened lawn, slow to recover. Do not try to mend shrinkage by pushing the pieces closer together, as this only disturbs newly-forming roots beneath. After soil repairs, continuous and very heavy watering is *essential*.

Avoid heavy rolling, and if irregularities do develop

a ◀

b ▶

c

d

e

f

g

correct *hollows* by sieving fine sandy soil over the surface, and *humps* by lifting the turf and scraping surplus soil from underneath. Do not apply strong fertilisers or weedkillers for at least twelve months. Regular close mowing will improve the lawn rapidly.

(*a*) Lay broad planks across the levelled surface, on which the wheelbarrow can roll. This is not only easier but also prevents the heavily-laden wheel from digging deeply into the raked soil. Do not carry many turves at once, and keep them towards the front of the wheelbarrow so that the weight is carried by the wheel, not by your arms.

(*b*) Unload the turves into piles near the working area. They are usually folded grass to grass with the roots outwards. Keep them this way until they are laid. Turves left folded for some days will turn yellow, but this will not permanently injure them. However, such treatment does tend to encourage any remaining weeds in the turf; clover in particular may become more vigorous.

(*c*) Treading always on boards, re-rake the ground to a fine tilth immediately before laying each turf.

(*d*) Good turf will withstand being pulled up from one end and lifted, rather like heavy carpet. Poor turf will collapse. It is more important that the roots be strong and grass blades healthy than that the grass should be particularly short. Most turf nowadays is cut by machines and should be even in thickness and therefore easy to lay.

(*e*) Simply unfold each turf and spread it flat. Guide pegs driven in as shown earlier help to make sure that the levels are kept correct.

(*f*) A square of timber fastened to the end of a post is useful for patting down the turves. Heavy ramming is not desirable. Just make sure that the turves are pressed closely against the soil.

(*g*) Add further rows, working inwards and 'bonding' the joints exactly as bricks are bonded in a wall. This staggering of joints helps the turf to knit together quickly.

(*h*) Continually check for level, using a long straight board set on your guide pegs and the turves already laid.

(*i*) Continue to add rows of turf, outlining the shapes of any beds required.

h

i

21

# THE IMPORTANT JOB OF
# DOUBLE DIGGING

For good growth of deep-rooting plants nothing is more important than careful preparation of the soil.

*Double digging* is one of the best methods for producing deep, rich soil for permanent beds of flowers, small shrubs, roses, soft fruit and vegetables. This is quite simple in principle but is not a quick operation. Do not attempt too much at a time. It is better to take several weekends over the digging of a large bed rather than get overtired and do a poor job.

The basic idea is to improve the condition of the soil below the top few inches. The upper 8–10in (20–25cm) of soil (*top soil*) is usually fairly fertile, but beneath it are layers of subsoil, which is much poorer and contains fewer plant foods. By digging rotted vegetation and fertilisers into this bottom layer you can improve the plants' chances of finding food when their roots reach down into it.

Double digging is also especially valuable on overgrown land with heavy weed or grass cover. This can be skimmed off and deeply buried where it will not re-grow but rot down to plant food.

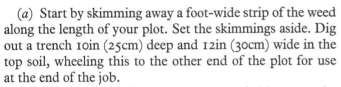

(*a*) Start by skimming away a foot-wide strip of the weed along the length of your plot. Set the skimmings aside. Dig out a trench 10in (25cm) deep and 12in (30cm) wide in the top soil, wheeling this to the other end of the plot for use at the end of the job.

(*b*) Simple double digging is done by forking over the base of the trench. This loosens up the subsoil and so improves the drainage. This alone will gradually produce a greater depth of fertile soil.

(*c*) Better still though, is to dig in fertilisers, particularly bulky organic kinds such as stable or farmyard manure with straw. Fork this deeply into the trench bottom.

(*d*) Skim away the weed on the next strip, adjacent to the trench. Do not take these skimmings away, but turn them upside down into the bottom of the trench and chop them up small. Add manure, and fork over as before.

(*e*) Next dig the top soil to 12in (30cm) back from the trench side, turning it over into the first trench. This soil will fill up the *first* trench and leave exposed the *second* one. The bottom of this second trench is then manured and forked.

Repeat this process right across the plot, using the grass and soil from the *first* trench to fill up the *last* one.

# THE CONTAINER REVOLUTION

It used to be a fact that few plants could be transplanted whilst in flower. All trees, shrubs, roses and many herbaceous plants were therefore put in during the late autumn, winter or early spring. Unfortunately these are often periods of unpleasant weather, with frostbound or waterlogged soil.

A revolution has now taken place in the growers' world by the widening use of *container growing*. Under this system plants are grown in tins, pots of waterproofed felt, or other containers. Within these they can develop to saleable size and they may be transferred bodily into the buyer's garden at any time of year without risk. Their roots will have filled the container and can be tapped out without disturbance. After planting they will continue to grow on without check. It is now possible to buy rose bushes, herbaceous plants, and indeed trees, whilst they are in full bloom. This is most helpful to those new gardeners who are unfamiliar with plants and who have only the vaguest idea of what a particular one may look like.

## BUYING

The best thing to do is to go to the nearest garden centre several times during spring and summer. There, everything from rock plants to trees can be seen at various stages of growth, their flower and leaf colours and shapes perfectly clear. Though container plants tend to be more expensive than those grown in open fields, most of us feel that this is more than compensated for by the pleasure of being able to go shopping for plants in bloom, bringing them home and putting them in without delay.

All the plants shown on these pages can now be bought container-grown. At the top of the page (*left*) is *Hosta*,

a

grown mainly for its large decorative leaves which can be seen to best advantage in the summer, when its much less impressive flowers are also on view. Below that is *Caltha*, with its masses of yellow blooms. Like *Hosta* this too is specially suited to moist areas near pools. *Bergenia* (*bottom left*) has large glossy leaves, and sheaves of pink flowers in summer.

That most popular of all plants, the rose, is available in containers and even a standard (*top right*) may be safely planted in full bloom. See that the stake provided is thoroughly secure in the ground, replacing it with a longer, stronger one if necessary. Below the standard rose is a photograph of dogwood (*Cornus*), one of the many large shrubs now also sold in containers, often the large whalehide pots described below.

## PLANTING

(*a*) The simplest container is an ordinary plastic pot and many small plants are grown in these. Planting is easy—simply withdraw them from the pot and the roots should hold together firmly.

(*b*) Place the root ball in the prepared hole.

(*c*) Draw more soil up level around it, pressing firmly until the plant is held securely. Remember to stake it, if necessary, against strong winds. Success is almost certain because the plant already has an actively growing root system which has not been disturbed.

(*d*) Whalehide looks like roofing felt made up into large plant pots. With these it is not always necessary to take the plant completely out. The felt will rot away once it is underground, but pull away the bottom of the pot before planting.

a

b

c

# GROWING SPECIMEN SHRUBS IN PLANTING PITS

All shrubs remain in position for a long time. They need deep rich soil, and this is best produced in large beds by the double-digging method described on page 22. Often, however, we wish to put a special shrub in an area where only shallow cultivation has been given—for example, on a lawn. The simplest solution here is to dig a planting pit. This gives all the advantages of deep cultivation without the labour of double digging a large area.

## PUTTING IN A RHODODENDRON

(*a*) The diameter of the pit depends on the ultimate size of the plant but should not be less than 2ft (60cm). First scoop out all the good top soil and set it aside.

(*b*) A well-made compost, with added general fertiliser, will provide years of future plant food. Tip a generous quantity into the pit.

(*c*) Dig it in deeply. This deep digging will both improve the drainage and provide reserves of plant food deep down in the soil.

(*d*) Granulated peat is especially valuable for rhododendrons, which like slightly acid soil, *without lime* (poisonous to rhododendrons and azaleas).

(*e*) This rhododendron has been supplied in a large polythene container that can easily be torn away.

(*f*) Rhododendrons make a solid root ball. Stand it in position on a bed of peat . . .

d

e

f

**g**

(*g*) . . . and fill up around the ball with more fine, peaty soil.

(*h*) Hold the plant securely whilst treading the soil firmly around the ball. This is most important. Firm planting is essential for the success of any shrub.

(*i*) Bring the soil up to the top of the root ball, ensuring that the plant is not buried deeper than it was in the pot.

**h** ◀

**i** ▶

**j** ▶

## WINTER PROTECTION

Where there is risk of severe winds it is best to protect valuable plants during their first winter at least.

(*j*) Three or four stakes driven in around the plant, and to the height of the plant, are all that is needed.

(*k*) Drape on two or three sides with sacking or polythene. Do not however completely cover the plant, which must have access to air and light even during winter.

**k**

# CHOOSING A HEDGE

Although hedges are less popular than formerly there are still many miles of new hedge planted each year. There are seven or eight main types which, over the years, have proved themselves to respond to close clipping with sturdy growth.

### GETTING IT THICK

A hedge may have three main functions: to keep out intruding dogs and children; to act as a screen; and to be a thing of beauty. It should also be simple to maintain.

Growing a hedge is a long job—some slow-growing varieties taking up to ten or fifteen years before they achieve a good height. In the commentary on the illustrations, speed of growth is indicated, but note that this does vary according to the type and condition of the soil, and the aspect and situation of the hedge.

It is a common mistake to force the hedge to grow too rapidly. This often results in a thin, sparsely filled base. To encourage rapid growth and thickening of a hedge, start by clipping early, immediately after planting in some cases, so that dormant buds further down the bushes will send out their stems. The only exception to this is beech, which tends to resent having its leading shoot trimmed. Do not cut short the upper tips of beech plants until they have reached the desired height of the hedge. Trim the side shoots though, to force the lower branches to thicken.

## COSTS AND OTHER CONSIDERATIONS

(a) Yew is slow growing at first and quite expensive, but eventually gives one of the best evergreen hedges. The leaves are poisonous to animals and the berries to children. It needs to be clipped only once or twice during the year.

(b) Holly is again very slow growing and therefore tends to be expensive. It is an excellent evergreen barrier hedge, being almost impenetrable when mature. Clipping is done only once a year. Golden varieties are weaker and slower to grow.

(c) Hornbeam (often mistaken for beech) is relatively quick in growth and not over-expensive. Although not evergreen, it retains its dead leaves throughout winter (as the beech does). It can never be trimmed to a really neat shape because of the size of the leaves, but makes a fine, rich green background for flower borders and rose beds. A single trim in the year is enough when mature.

There are several plants popularly called cypress, including *Cupressus*, *Chamaecyparis* and *Thuja*. All are similar in appearance and rapidly form a tall hedge. They can be planted when already several feet tall, but this is expensive. Small plants are cheap and development is rapid: in mild areas *Cupressus macrocarpa* gives a tall hedge with surprising speed. Some varieties of *Thuja* can be clipped finely, but clipping is not needed at all in many cases, the plants keeping a slim, erect growth.

(d) Laurel is one of the quickest growing evergreen hedges; the variegated types tend to be slower to develop. It is fairly expensive, especially if large bushes are bought; but as early growth is swift this is not necessary. Laurel withstands severe clipping well, but looks better when allowed a looser growth and clipped only two or three times a year.

(e) Privet—especially the golden variety—although used excessively is still a very satisfactory evergreen hedge. Rapid in growth, takes a hard clip if necessary, or will form a looser hedge with attractively perfumed white flowers. It is tolerant of neglect and grows even in the heart of towns. One disadvantage is its habit of sending out roots for many feet on either side, which can deplete the soil of nearby flower beds. A tidy hedge needs regular, frequent clipping: once a fortnight throughout the summer is not too much.

(f) Beech is less expensive than most hedge plants and not too slow in growth, especially on well-drained ground containing lime. When mature, the colour variations throughout the year are most attractive: from a very pale spring green to the rich green of summer, then turning into the golds and russets of autumn. Often the last leaves remain throughout winter, making the hedge as good a screen as an evergreen. An August clipping is all that is normally required. The copper beeches are very fine.

(g) Box is a slow evergreen hedge with small leaves which look very well indeed if tightly clipped. Not poisonous. If bought tall, plants are expensive.

Other hedge material includes hawthorn (cheap, rapid-growing but bare of leaves in winter), *Berberis* and some kinds of *Prunus*, which like beech produce a coloured hedge. Hawthorn is perhaps more suitable for country gardens.

## PLANTING

Planting hedges is not difficult but always prepare the soil by deep trenching. A hedge will remain in position for many years and if the roots find rich soil immediately beneath them they will have less tendency to creep out sideways into the adjoining beds.

(*a*) Nearly all hedges are best planted 'staggered' in two rows, with the plants in the front row placed in the gaps between those in the rear row.

(*b*) First stretch two strings along the line of the hedge.

(*c*) Next stand the hedge plants in position, spacing them correctly, according to their type.

(*d*) Draw the soil carefully around their roots, working i well between the finer roots.

(*e*) Finally fill up the trench level so that the hedge plant are roughly at the same depth as they were in the nursery Tread them firm and in exposed sites support the youns plants against wind by posts and wires stretched along.

(*f*) Trimming hedges is often done incorrectly, with vertical sides. This tends to cause the bottom of the hedge t become thin. Correctly trimmed hedges have sides that slope inwards so that the top is narrower than the base. Hedge clipped like this retain leaves right down to the ground Trim newly-planted deciduous hedges lightly level, re moving roughly one-third of the uppermost stems. Thi causes them to branch out.

An exception is beech, which should not have its leadins shoots trimmed until it has reached the height required.

# TREES IN SMALL GARDENS

A small modern garden is no place to grow forest giants. Instead, choose small varieties of flowering or foliage trees. The choice is wide. Here we can give samples of only the most popular kinds. All these are vigorous and generally flower well. It pays, however, to look around your local nurseries to find unusual varieties suited to your soil and climate.

## FROST, RAIN, WIND AND THE NEW TREE

The critical time is at planting. Most trees are supplied dug from the nursery and delivered during their dormant season between late autumn and early spring. Do not plant them if the soil is frozen or waterlogged after heavy rain but leave them, still in their wrappings, in a cool garage or shed. Alternatively cover the roots temporarily with soil in a sheltered part of the garden.

Plant in open weather when the soil is moist and hard frost unlikely.

Staking is important. Wind can loosen roots and even snap unstaked trunks. A single stake, to which the trunk is tied in several places, will usually be enough. In very exposed positions two stakes, one inclined at an angle against the prevailing wind, may be needed.

Make sure the fastening does not chafe the trunk. Modern plastic straps gradually release themselves as the tree increases in size.

a

b ◀

## TYPES TO CHOOSE FROM

**Evergreen:** retain their leaves all the year round, examples are pines, firs and cypresses.

**Deciduous:** lose their leaves in winter.

**Weeping:** of the familiar umbrella shape, branch tips in some cases hanging down almost to touch the soil; pleasant in appearance even when not in leaf.

**Erect:** branches flung almost vertically up to the sky, forming tall, narrow columns—the poplar is a familiar example; some flowering cherry varieties grow in this way and make beautiful garden features.

**Coloured:** justifiably popular—often gayer in colour than the most vigorous flowering trees and brilliant in autumn; *Acer* (maple) and certain kinds of *Prunus* are well-known examples.

**Flowering:** cherries, almond, laburnum and lilacs are popular.

c

d ▶

## LOOK FOR THESE IN GARDEN CENTRES AND NURSERIES

When choosing trees visit garden centres and nurseries during the flowering season. You can then decide which plants suit your particular need and the nurseryman will advise whether they are likely to do well in your own area.

(*a*) A rare variety of weeping cedar tree is *Cedrus atlantica glauca*. It is slow-growing but graceful even when young.

(*b*) Weeping willow (*Salix babylonica*) will grow in even fairly dry situations. It is often best on a lawn, where its graceful form can display itself well, but may need pruning in later years, to keep it within bounds.

(*c*) The Camperdown elm (*Ulmus glabra* 'Camperdownii') is a weeping variety which forms a compact head with very large, impressive leaves.

(*d*) The weeping birch (*Betula pendula* 'Youngii') is most popular for small gardens. It never becomes really large.

(*e*) Of the evergreens, firs are the most suitable for small gardens. This is an ordinary Christmas tree (*Picea abies*). If bought with roots from a nursery it is fairly rapid in growth.

(*f*) Acers (maples) come in many varieties. This is Golden Acer, grown as a small tree.

(*g*) Other acers have very finely divided leaves and develop more like large bushes. They are slow growing and often have richly coloured leaves, turning to glorious gold, yellow and red in autumn.

e

f

g

a

b

# PLANTING A TREE

## ESSENTIALS

A tree remains for many years in its original position, so the ground in which it grows must be fertile and well-drained. If the soil has too little plant food, is waterlogged or very hard, development will be slow, or the tree may die.

It is essential that the newly planted tree should be strongly staked to prevent rocking in the wind, which hinders the formation of new fine roots. A strong wind of course could blow an unsupported tree right over.

Finally, when the actual planting is done, the soil must be packed very firmly amongst and between the roots. Loose planting is one of the most frequent causes of failure with trees and shrubs. The tree should ideally be held as firmly as it was in its original home in the nursery.

## A WAITING PIT

Preparation of planting pits for trees should be completed well in advance, so that the manure will have time to improve the texture and fertility of the soil.

(a) To protect the grass or bed near the planting pit, spread a sheet of thick polythene over the area adjoining the planting hole. This must be at least 3ft (1m) across, more if possible.

c
◀

d
▶

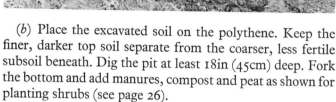

(b) Place the excavated soil on the polythene. Keep the finer, darker top soil separate from the coarser, less fertile subsoil beneath. Dig the pit at least 18in (45cm) deep. Fork the bottom and add manures, compost and peat as shown for planting shrubs (see page 26).

(c) Always place a supporting stake *before* planting the tree. Otherwise you are likely to damage the roots when driving it in. Make sure it goes down as far as possible and tread the soil firm about its base.

## IN WITH CARE

(d) Stand the tree in position, keeping its trunk parallel with the supporting post. Spread fine soil from your top-soil heap about the finer roots of the tree, treading it firmly. Roots damaged in transplanting must be cut cleanly off—splits lead to disease.

(e) Remember that all plants extract their food from the soil via the finest roots, not through the coarser ones, so it is important to work soil closely amongst them and not leave large empty spaces.

(f) Before completing the back-filling of the hole, flood the entire bottom with several gallons of water (unless the soil is already thoroughly soaking). This will settle fine particles of soil against the roots.

(g) Finally complete the back-filling, treading the soil *very firmly indeed* so that the roots are strongly held. A top inch or so of soil should however be left loose and friable.

(h) Finally bind the trunk of the tree firmly, but without chafing, to its stake at several points. You can use cord and sacking, but there are commercial plastic ties which are better. These expand as the tree grows and will not cut into the bark.

After frosty spells retread the roots to ensure that soil remains in contact with them.

# PATHS AND PATIOS

### CHOOSING MATERIALS

Paving for paths and patios is the most expensive material in the garden: a few yards of good sandstone slabs may cost many pounds. On the other hand, areas of gravel are cheap. Bricks bought secondhand fall between these extremes.

It is important when planning your garden to choose carefully the materials to be used, taking into account cost, appearance, wearing capacity, and ease of laying and subsequent maintenance (a consideration not to be overlooked).

Solid cast concrete is certainly the most hardwearing of all but is little used. Its very strength may be a disadvantage since it is difficult to alter as the garden develops. It also has a grey, dull appearance. However, a garden in modern style might call for formal, rectangular concrete slabs, whilst a more traditional garden would be better served with pathways of bricks or even wood.

## COST, LABOUR AND UPKEEP

(a) **Gravel.** An area of gravel is simple to lay out over a foundation of several inches of well-rammed, broken stones. It is simply scattered over the surface, raked flat and rolled. The gravel may be loose stone chips or river-bed pebbles; there are certain kinds available containing fine particles which after mixing with water form a surface similar to concrete, though not so hard. Gravel is cheap, easy to handle, easy to lay or alter later. However, weeds will often be a problem, and the edges will need to be supported with kerbs.

(b) **Asphalt.** Over a hard foundation, cold asphalt is not difficult to lay. It is available in black or in a number of colours, and is bought in bags ready to spread. Simply rake it out and roll it. A heavy garden roller is usually sufficient for this although you can hire power-driven rollers for large areas. If a thick surface is required a preliminary 2in (5cm) layer of tarred limestone chips is both strengthening and reduces costs. The work must be done rapidly in one session to avoid joints in the surface, which are difficult to conceal. Asphalt is somewhat dearer than gravel but similarly requires kerbs. Maintenance is less of a problem though weeds often creep into the edges.

(c) **Slabs.** Slabs of concrete or stone, though expensive, are probably the most popular of all garden materials. Concrete has the advantages of lower price and regularity of thickness. Most slabs are laid on a bed of sand over well-rammed foundations of broken stones. Some mortar may be needed under the joints but otherwise little cement is called for. Slab paths may be altered fairly easily as the garden design progresses. Weeds need not be a problem and of course such paths require no kerbs. The work is moderately heavy, but can be spread over many working days.

(d) **Crazy paving.** Random shapes of sandstone or limestone are often available cheaply near quarries. Properly handled they make a pleasing path, especially for an older style of garden. Stone thickness varies a good deal. Thin material is best bedded on cement but thicker sorts can be laid on sand. This is a simple operation. Creeping plants may be grown in the joints.

(e) **Bricks.** Secondhand bricks especially, which have weathered to pleasing colours, are in may ways an ideal garden path material. They can be laid easily and quickly on a simple sand bed; are equally easy to alter later; withstand a good deal of wear and can also be laid in curves or with a curved surface. Their pleasing colours and texture blend with most types of garden.

(f) **Wood.** This is an unusual garden path material but can be very attractive. Made with round, short logs, such paths and patios are soft under foot yet surprisingly hard-wearing. Provided the logs are properly treated against rot they will last for many years.

37

a

# ALWAYS START AT THE BOTTOM—PATH FOUNDATIONS

No path can be stronger than its foundation; it is important too that these be well-drained, otherwise water tends to accumulate at the path edges. The central pipe drain shown here can be linked in with the other garden drains to form a complete system. A path on good foundations will last for years, dry rapidly after rain, and contribute to the overall draining of the garden.

(*a*) Excavate the path area at least 8in (20cm) deep, sloping its base gently towards the centre. Rake a shallow bed of sand over the entire area. Press down into the middle of this 3in (7.5cm) clay pipes, touching each other, but *not* cemented.

(*b*) Pack large broken rubble around the pipes and over the trench base. Ram this well without disturbing the pipes.

(*c*) Cover this rubble with finer material and top the whole with 2in (5cm) of coarse sand. Any surfacing material (except solid cast concrete) can be bedded on this.

b

c

# GRAVEL PATHS

Nothing could be easier than laying out a gravel path. On top of the stone foundations simply tip the stone chips into place and rake them level. If you use the self-setting type, which contains a fine powder, flood this with water and then roll the path well. One of the advantages of gravel paths is that the surface can be re-raked and rolled to remove weeds and to give a renewed appearance. Additional gravel can be added year by year to keep the surface sound.

# ASPHALT PATHS AND SURFACING

Cold asphalt is laid over a firm, well-rammed surface. Kerbs are needed at the edges. They are best made of concrete, but flat stones on edge can be used, or bricks. All these must be cemented in first, and allowed to set for a week (see pages 123–5 for a method of casting your own kerbing blocks). Wood strips, soaked in preservative and mounted on short stout pegs can also be used, but will not last so long. The asphalt is bought in bags, tipped out, raked level, and then rolled flat. A garden roller is usually adequate, but powered kinds can be hired for big jobs. The paths can be used after only an hour or two.

Asphalt is also useful for laying over a poor, existing path. If this is of solid concrete or slabs, paint the surface with a special primer, obtainable from the asphalt suppliers.

White or coloured stone chippings may be scattered over the final surface and rolled down into it as a decorative finish.

# LAYING OUT SLAB PATIOS

### BEDDING AND SITING

Slabs of concrete and of stone are laid in much the same way. The strongest method of all is to embed them in a 4–5in (10–12.5cm) layer of wet concrete. This is best bought ready-mixed, spread out evenly, rammed, and the stones pressed into the still-wet surface.

However, such an operation is expensive and calls for a good deal of labour. It is practically impossible for one person to tackle any substantial area. Moreover, concrete is very difficult to alter later.

The method shown on pages 42–3 uses slabs laid on sand beds. This is quite strong enough for normal wear, and gives a fine well-drained surface which quickly dries after rain.

Cement underneath the joints is not strictly necessary with skilful work, but does simplify the job somewhat. The mortar takes up any irregularities in the sand bed and makes levelling easier.

Remember always to slope patios *away* from the house and, in particular, make sure the house damp proof course is *above* any paving adjoining the wall. Otherwise, water will find its way up from underneath the slabs and create rising damp in the house.

### THE SLABS

Commercially produced slabs are made in different sizes that are planned to fit together accurately. For example, slabs may be made in squares or rectangles having sides 9in, 18in and 27in long (the corresponding metric sizes being 25cm, 50cm and 75cm). They can therefore be arranged in regular patterns without cutting.

The largest size that should be used for home work is 
ft 6in × 1ft 6in (or 75 × 50cm). Larger slabs weigh more 
han a hundredweight each, are difficult to manoeuvre and 
o not look so good in small gardens. At the other extreme, 
he very small slabs 9 × 12in (or 25 × 35cm) square, should 
e used only in small numbers and as part of patterns based 
n bigger slabs. Used alone, they are difficult to fit together 
ccurately unless they are laid on a solid concrete bed.

Before ordering materials draw out the area to scale. Then 
rrange on this plan cardboard squares and rectangles cut to 
he scale of the slab sizes available. Adjust the positions of 
arge and small slabs to establish the precise number 
equired of each size. Mark the final arrangement on the 
lan that is to be used when the work is being done and the 
orrect sizes can then be laid at each stage. It pays always to 
rder a few extra slabs in each size because it is difficult to 
ay a large area of paving without cracking a few. Broken 
nes can still be saved and used elsewhere or broken up 
urther and set in cement as crazy paving.

Paving with curved edges calls for slab cutting. This need 
resent no problems. The technique is shown on pages 
o–1. Raise the adjoining soil level with or slightly above the 
aving to conceal the rough-cut edges. Kerbs for curved 
reas can be made by cutting ordinary 3ft (1m) kerbs into 
ft (30cm) lengths and carefully cementing these together.

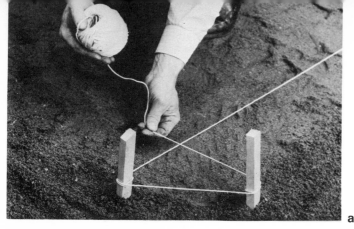

## CEMENT POINTS METHOD

(*a*) Foundations of 4–6in (10–15cm) well-rammed rubble are desirable, topped with a level bed of coarse sand 2in (5cm) thick. Tread and rake this level. Drive in two pegs just *outside* each corner to carry the guide strings that will outline the edges of the paving. Loop string around the pegs as shown here so that the corner is clearly outlined.

(*b*) Fit all corner pegs, checking that they and the sand bed are as level as possible (see the section on levelling, pages 16–17).

(*c*) On square or rectangular areas start laying the slabs in the corners. Place trowels of mortar (mixed four parts of sand and one of cement, see page 109) under each corner where the slab is to rest.

(*d*) Lower the slab into place and tap it down with the *wooden* handle of a heavy hammer. (Do not strike slabs with metal tools or they may crack.) Align the slab edges exactly along the two guide-strings.

(*e*) Check its lie with a long spirit-level. Where a sloping area is to be laid, fix packing beneath the lower end of level, thick enough to give the desired slope when level bubble is central.

(*f*) Smooth away the cement which was squeezed out from beneath the two outer edges of the slab.

(*g*) When the four corner slabs are laid they act as guides for rapid laying of the rest of the slabs. It is important therefore that they should be perfectly level with each other. Check this by putting a long straight board across from corner to corner and side to side, with a spirit-level resting on its top edge.

(*h*) Add more slabs in the way already described. Check that they are flat by laying the straight board across the corner guide slabs. Remember, too, to check *diagonally*, or you may find you have a hollow in the middle of the paving which would cause puddles after rain.

(*i*) Once the cement has set (after about a week) scatter coarse sand or a dry sand-and-cement mixture over the entire surface of the slabs and brush this well down into the joints.

(*j*) Flood the surface with water to wash the sand well down into them. Repeat this operation as necessary. The result will be a flat and accurately fitted area of slabs which will give many years of service.

g

h

i

◀

j

▶

# SETTS IN PAVING

## IMPROVE YOUR PATIO

Large areas of concrete slab paving often look uninteresting. A good way to improve their appearance is to take out a number of the slabs and then to fill the gaps with much smaller blocks. Broken slabs can be replaced like this. The cubes of stone known as setts are ideal. Setts are cut from very hard stone, usually granite, and are used for roads and paths all over the world. You can sometimes buy them from local authorities or builders' merchants.

## LAYING SETTS IS SIMPLE

(*a*) It looks best if the spaces in the paving are not exactly equal, but rather irregular—some small, some large. Move the slabs apart if there is space, or lift a few right out. In areas of similar-sized slabs, you can cut some smaller, using the methods shown on pages 50–1.

(*b*) Setts are thicker than slabs, so dig out the foundation a little deeper than their thickness. This allows for the mortar bed that is to be placed under them.

(*c*) Setts come in different sizes, so first arrange the required number on the paving beside your hole. This ensures that you will not be delayed whilst you search for the right sizes.

(*d*) Mix a fairly dry mortar of one part of cement to three parts of sand and spread a layer roughly 1in (2.5cm) deep over the bottom of the space.

(*e*) Stand the setts on this mortar and hammer them down until they are level with the surrounding paving.

(*f*) Leave $\frac{1}{4}$in (6mm) spaces between the setts. This gives a very much better appearance than if they are packed tightly together.

b

c

d

f

(g) Even single rows of setts at intervals can look very effective.

(h) Let the mortar dry for a week and then scatter plain sand over the surface.

(i) Brush this well down into the gaps between the setts. The sand locks the setts together. Let it settle for a day or two.

(j) In dry weather, water the paving to wash the sand in.

(k) Repeat sanding and brushing until the joints remain full.

**a** ◀

**b** ▶

**c** ◀

**d** ▶

## AND MORE SETTS

(*a*) Setts make unusual kerbstones, or several rows of them can widen a path that is too narrow.

(*b*) Complete paths can be made too, laid like the brick paths shown on pages 52–3.

(*c*) Where trees grow in paved areas, setts laid up to the trunk can be removed easily as the trunk develops.

(*d*) Cast concrete blocks may be used instead of real stone setts. Often these are shaped to interlock with each other.

(*e*) Small setts laid in complex patterns are a pleasant feature of many European towns.

**e**

# NATURAL STONE PAVING

You can buy sandstone and limestone slabs in pleasing irregular shapes. This natural stone paving is most popular for gardens. It is the cheapest kind to buy and does not require a great deal of skill to lay.

The strongest method is to embed the slabs into concrete but this is time-consuming and expensive. Cement points (see page 42) can also serve, but call for rather a lot of mortar, which again is expensive and takes time and labour to mix.

A much simpler method, where traffic is not heavy, is to lay the stones directly upon a bed of plain sand. First, take out a foundation roughly 9in (22cm) deep and ram in a 4in (10cm) layer of stone and brick rubble. On top of this, spread a bed of coarse concreting sand about 2in (5cm) deep, on which the stones can be laid.

(*a*) In any delivery of natural stone there will be different sized pieces. To get the best effect, sort *before* laying and pick out the largest pieces for the edges of the path or patio.

(*b*) Fix the stones permanently by applying pressure to their top surfaces and hammering the sand under all their edges with a long-nosed or mason's hammer. A board laid across helps to prevent the sand-bed being trampled.

(*c*) A spirit-level laid across from edge to edge will check that your path is being laid perfectly flat. Use the smaller stones for filling up the centre. If necessary you can embed the smallest pieces in a mortar (using a mixture of one part cement to every four parts of sand). The smaller the piece the more mortar is required.

(*d*) Minor shaping to fit can be easily done with the chisel-back of the mason's hammer (see pages 50–1 for more details about stone and slab shaping).

(*e*) Fill all gaps between the stones with sand, brushed well down into the joints.

(*f*) Finally flood the surface with water to wash the sand down into the joints.

Paths of this kind do not take long to lay, will last a fair number of years and are easy to repair. If instead of plain sand you use a sand-soil mixture this will enable plants to be grown attractively between the stones (see photograph above).

a

b

c

d

e

f

a

# CUTTING STONE AND CONCRETE SLABS TO SHAPE

## A STRAIGHT CUT

(*a*) Rest the slab being cut on a heap of fine soft soil, pressing it firmly down into this. Make sure that it remains embedded securely all the time you are chiselling. Mark the cutting line with chalk or soft pencil.

(*b*) Use a broad chisel to cut a very shallow scratch. It need not be more than about $\frac{1}{16}$ in (2mm) deep, but must be *even* in depth and perfectly straight.

(*c*) Chisel across the *thickness* of the slab also, at both ends of your cutting line.

(*d*) Now mark the rear of the slab, ready for making a scratch across there too.

(*e*) Use a heavy hammer to strike the face of the slab firmly but not violent blows up and down the crack. The ringing tone of the blows will change to dull thuds.

(*f*) Even-textured slabs such as concrete or sandstone should split perfectly straight, but any small irregularities can be easily chiselled away afterwards.

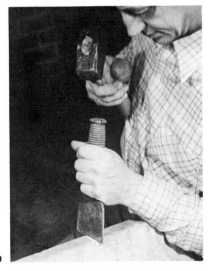

b

c

d ◀

e ◀

f

h ◀

g ◀

i ▶

## EXTERIOR CURVES

(*g*) Mark the curve, then cut away most of the waste with a straight cut, as shown.

(*h*) Use narrower chisels to cut along the curve, making your scratch much deeper than for a straight cut.

(*i*) Continue to chisel along *both* faces of the slab until the pieces of waste flake away.

(*j*) Finish the curve by standing the slab on edge between you knees and chiselling *away* from the corners (to avoid breaking them), till the slab is worked . . .

(*k*) . . . to an even curve.

## INTERIOR CURVES

(*l*) These, needed for example around drainpipes, require patience. Mark the curve on both faces of the slab.

(*m*) Then with a *very sharp* chisel start in the middle of the waste to chip this away in small pieces, on both faces.

(*n*) Work inwards to cut a shallow trench but *do not go right up to your cutting line.*

(*o*) Gradually work away all the waste, chiselling inwards from the cutting line and taking away only small chips.

(*p*) Continue widening the curve until the right shape . . .

(*q*) . . . is reached.

j

k

l

m

n

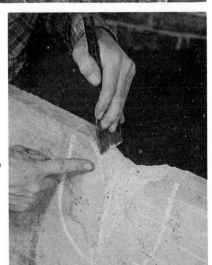

o

p

q

51

# PAVING IN BRICKS

## THE VIRTUES OF BRICK

Brick paths have a pleasing texture which blends well with most kinds of gardens. Not only are they easy to lay but, perhaps equally important, are easy to alter later. Where possible, use old bricks that have a pleasant, weathered appearance. Avoid raw, bright-red new kinds.

To keep paths dry it is best if they are 'crowned', the centre of them being made a little higher than their edges and sloping in an even curve to each side. This kind of path can easily be constructed with bricks. Bricks with 'frogs' on their faces to retain the mortar must be set *on edge*.

## MAKING A CROWNED PATH

The bricks are set on a 2in (5cm) foundation of rammed sand. Preferably also there should be a 4–5in (10–12cm) layer of broken stones underneath. In dry parts of the garden however, and where traffic is light, the sand can be used alone, over well-rammed soil. Rake it out reasonably smoothly, then tread it firm, with a rough crowning.

(*a*) For an accurate crown you need a template. This is a length of stiff wood with blocks nailed at both ends and a further strip of thinner wood nailed between to form a curve. Make this template the exact width of your path, and the curve roughly $1\frac{1}{4}$in deep for every yard of width (4cm for each metre of width).

(*b*) Press it, curved face down, on the sand and draw it along to give an evenly curved top surface.

(*c*) Pat the sand firm and solid with the template.

(*d*) When working on sand always use a short length of board. Lay a strip of mortar down *one edge only* of the path and spread it evenly with the tip of a trowel.

(*e*) Press in a first row of bricks as a kerb. Lay these flat and spaced about $\frac{1}{4}$in (6mm) apart.

(*f*) Tap them down lightly into the mortar, using the handle of a tool. Never strike a brick directly with metal.

(*g*) When you have laid about 1yd (1m) of path kerbing make a very thin mortar of one part cement, one part sand and enough water to make it creamy. Pour this mixture over the surface of the sand.

(*h*) Spread it out evenly, roughly $\frac{1}{4}$in (6mm) thick.

(*i*) Space the bricks evenly on the still wet cement, working as rapidly as possible in a pre-planned pattern.

(*j*) Work across the path until you reach the opposite edge. Then use stronger mortar, as before, to support the outer kerb-bricks. Make minor adjustments to the level of the bricks with a hammer, but interpose a piece of wood.

(*k*) Use your template across the top of the bricks to check that the curve is correct. Finally scatter a layer of plain sand over the surface of the path, brushing and watering this well down into all joints, as shown on page 49.

a

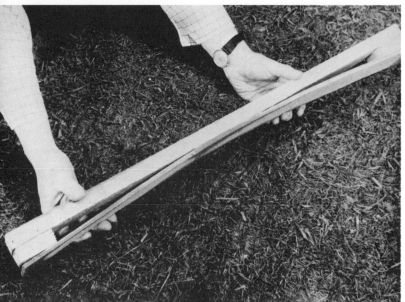

b

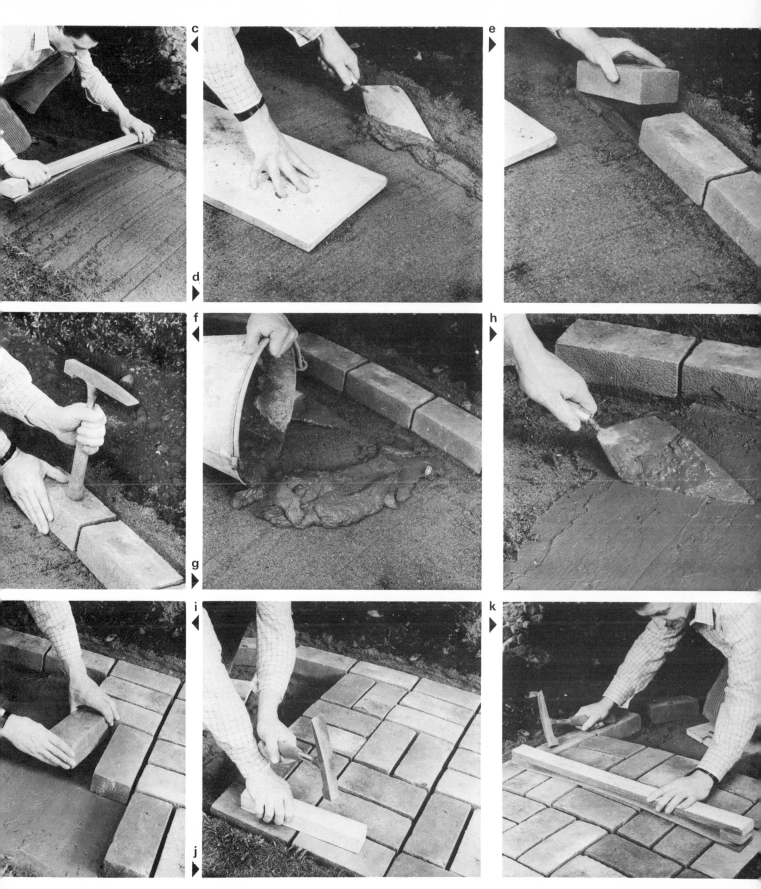

# BRICKS AND BLOCKS

By combining two different materials for paths or patios you can often achieve unusual effects. This requires some caution because not all materials mix well together; it is hard, for example, to blend natural stone with grey concrete blocks. But textured concrete can often be used with bricks to form attractive paths.

First prepare foundations and a sand bed as for the crowned brick path.

(*a*) Start by laying a few rows of bricks right down the middle of the path. Space them about $\frac{1}{4}$in (6mm) apart and tap them firmly down into the sand. Add more sand at the sides because the concrete slabs to be put there are thinner than bricks. Spread this sand in position, and smooth it out flat and firm. A dry sand/cement mixture (four parts of sand to one of cement) is even better.

(*b*) A good slab size is $9 \times 18$in ($22 \times 45$cm). This fits in well with brick sizes. Lay the slabs on the sand bed at the side of the bricks.

(*c*) Hammer the sand firmly under their edges till the slabs no longer rock.

(*d*) Scatter more dry-mix over the surface.

(*e*) Brush it down into the joints. Water sprayed over the job will help the sand/cement mix to set like a light mortar.

At the edges of the path, bring the soil up flush with the slab edges to help stop them sliding outwards.

a

b

c

**d**

**e**

**a**

## VARIATIONS IN PATTERN

Brick path patterns can be varied by the use of half bricks and other materials such as tiles.

Here we see how to make a decorative corner piece for the angle where two paths meet.

(*a*) Mark out the square and in a hole in the centre set a round drainpipe vertically, with its top a brick's thickness above the sand. Arrange around this half-bricks, with intervening rows of roofing tiles on edge.

(*b*) Check constantly, with a straight piece of wood and a spirit-level, that the brick tops are approximately flat.

(*c*) As you go along fill up the joints with sand or dry-mix. Soil for plants can be inserted in the drainpipe and in spaces specially left. Thyme is specially suitable, being perfumed and having no objection to being trodden on.

**b**
▶

**c**
▶

# PATHS IN WOOD

Log paths last a surprising number of years; they are comfortable underfoot, not difficult to make, and are particularly suited to the more 'natural' type of garden.

(*a*) Remove the bark from the logs using knife, spokeshave or shaping tool (shown here) so that the wood can be soaked with preservative. Rustic pole is used here, but any logwood will serve.

(*b*) Saw the logs into 8in (20cm) lengths.

(*c*) Dip every length in a reliable wood preservative. Creosote is effective and cheap in five gallon drums. Ideally they should remain in soak for several days: a trench lined with uncut polythene makes a temporary bath.

(*d*) Excavate the top soil from the path area to a depth of 10in (25cm). Rammed stone foundations, though desirable, are not usually necessary for log paths.

(*e*) Rake an even 2in (5cm) bed of coarse concreting sand over the foundation.

(*f*) Stand the logs upright and touching each other over the surface of the pathway.

(*g*) Use a hammer to tap them down level.

(*h*) Scatter more sand over the surface and brush this well down between every log. Flush over with water and repeat the sanding until they are held firmly.

(*i*) The tips of the logs should finally project $\frac{1}{4}$in (6mm) above the sand.

(*j*) Steps are easily made by using rows of somewhat longer logs to form the risers. The treads must be especially well rammed in. Where the steps are likely to get a great deal of wear it is better to embed the base of the logs in concrete.

Sawn rectangular timber can also be used in exactly the same way, cut off in 8in (20cm) lengths and set vertically (see photograph on the left).

a

b

c

# THE ART OF FENCING

The fence is usually the largest wooden structure in the garden. There are many different types but, as timber is expensive, light openwork structures are often chosen. The disadvantages of these are that they may not wear long and that they give little privacy.

Posts and rails are the basis of most fences, including the well-known 'ranch style'. By adding planks, vertical or horizontal, the fences are made progressively stronger. For complete privacy the solid plank fence of overlapped vertical planks is unbeatable, but expensive. Panels mounted on posts are cheaper but effective and may be made at home with great savings in cost.

## A FENCE IS AS GOOD AS ITS POSTS

Whatever the fence type, its strength ultimately depends entirely on its *posts* and the way in which these are embedded in the soil. Concrete is not always essential. Where the fence is not in an exposed position it is enough if the posts are sunk 18–24in (45–60cm) into well-rammed soil. But in light soil or windy positions, tall fences must have concrete around the bases of the posts and brought up above soil level.

(*a*) There are many methods of preserving wood. Quite a good protection can be given by burning the base of each post black in an open fire. The charred timber retards the entry of rot fungus. The most popular method is to use liquid preservative. Take care to coat the end-grain of wood thoroughly. This is where attack most often starts. Soaking for some days is better than brushing. Commercially impregnated timber is very good, but much more expensive.

The life of fence-posts of natural timber such as rustic pole can be greatly extended simply by erecting them *upside down*, the opposite way from which they grew in the tree. This is easily done with rustic poles, which taper from bottom to top. Place them thicker end *up* and rot will be considerably delayed.

(*b*) Concrete for posts must not be wet. Some moisture will be absorbed from the soil. A mixture of one part cement, two parts sand and three parts gravel will be found about right, but is not critical.

a

b

c

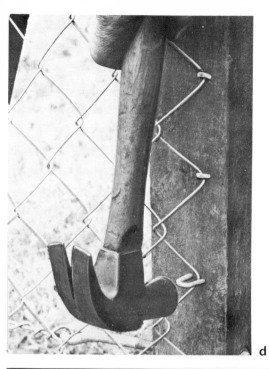

(*c*) Bring the concrete up above ground and slope it away from the posts to prevent water gathering near the wood. Slope post tops too (see page 66).

## NETTING

(*d*) Most houses already have at least a simple fence of wire, but netting may easily be added to keep out animals and children. Fasten it to the posts with staples. If diamond mesh fencing is used nail *every single loop* or it will tend to unravel. Plastic mesh is excellent, practically undestructible, and requires no maintenance at all.

## THE SIMPLE RAIL

(*e*) The simplest method of making a rail fence is to screw the plank rails directly to the face of each post. Thick wood-screws are needed, at least twice as long as the thickness of the rail.

(*f*) Good appearance depends on accuracy of alignment and careful jointing (see page 60) and painting. Any irregularity looks amateurish.

d

e

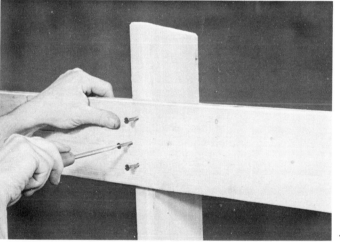

f

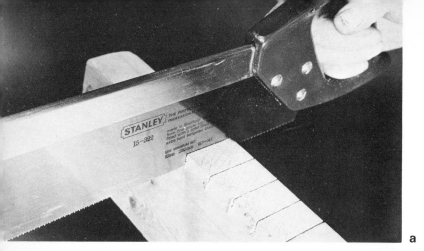

# RANCH-STYLE FENCING

## EMBEDDING THE CROSS PLANKS

For the true ranch-style fence it is better to embed the cross planks into the post. This jointing vastly increases it strength and improves its appearance. It takes extra time, o course, but is not technically too difficult.

(*a*) Mark the width of the cross plank on the front face o each post. Shade the waste with pencil and make sever saw cuts down into the wood nearly as *deep as the cross rail* thick.

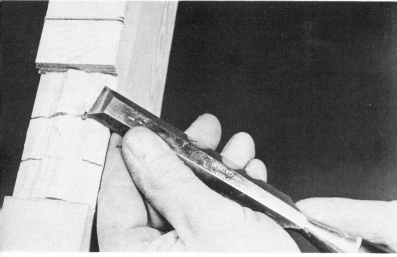

(*b*) Chisel from each side to remove the waste and leav a flat-bottomed 'trench'.

(*c*) Into this the cross rail is fitted.

(*d*) Woodscrews are driven through pre-drilled holes i the rail into the post behind.

(*e*) Fill the screw heads with sealer and give several coat of paint.

## JOINING RAILS

(*f*) Most long cross rails will need to be jointed end-to end. Use *scarf joints* for maximum strength and neatnes Cut the rail end off at a shallow angle and screw it to the post

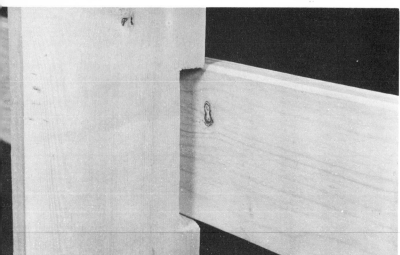

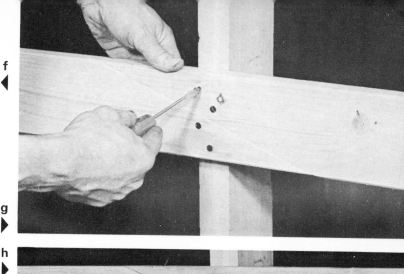

(*g*) Cut the adjoining rail at the opposite angle and screw it above the first.

(*h*) Drive long, thin screws vertically through the tapering ends of each rail to hold them firmly together. After filling and painting, such joints are practically invisible.

## A TALLER FENCE

(*i*) Where something taller is needed, you can erect a three-rail fence and then nail planks 4in (10cm) wide alternately front and rear of the rails. This gives a pleasing effect but of course is not peep-proof.

a

b

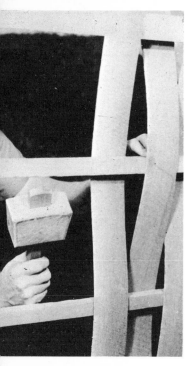

c

d

# FOR PRIVACY

## WEAVE YOUR OWN FENCING

There is a type of woven fencing that you can build directly on to posts and rails. The *vertical-woven fence* shown here is easy to make, relatively cheap, and pleasant in appearance. It is also very easily repaired.

It consists of horizontal rails between which thin planks of wood are woven. This last material is roughly $4 \times \frac{1}{4}$in ($10 \times 1$cm), and may have to be specially ordered. Few woodyards stock the size. Treat all the wood with preservative *before* erection.

(*a*) First screw to the fence posts four or more horizontal rails of wood about $1\frac{1}{2} \times 1$in ($4 \times 2.5$cm) in section. Space them 9in (22cm) to 12in (30cm) apart.

(*b*) Next, slide lengths of the weaving plank vertically downwards between the rails, weaving them under and over alternately. A wooden mallet is useful to tap them gently into place.

(*c*) Use the mallet then to drive the weaving planks sideways so that they butt firmly up against each other.

(*d*) The resulting fence is elegant in appearance and suitable for gardens of any style.

Fences on slopes are made similarly. Be sure that both posts and weaving planks are kept *vertical*.

## OR CHOOSE OVERLAP

(*e*) Though expensive, vertical overlap gives total privacy. The treated planks, usually 6–8in wide (15–20cm), are brought up to overlap each other. Some timber yards stock planks thinner on one edge, which are economical for this type of fence.

(*f*) Oval nails are driven through the overlap.

(*g*) The result is an almost unclimbable solid fence.

e

g

f

# FENCING WITH PANELS

The simplest form of solid panel fencing, and one of the cheapest, is *horizontal overlap*. These panels an be made of thin wood approximately $4 \times \frac{1}{4}$in ($10 \times 1$cm), with framing about $1 \times 1\frac{1}{2}$in ($2.5 \times 4$cm) in section. Any straight-grained, reasonably strong softwood can be used, and treated with preservative or paint.

We show here how to make a panel $6 \times 3$ft ($2 \times 1$m) in area, but the size can be adjusted within wide limits.

(*a*) Lay two framing pieces, each 3ft (1m) long, 6ft (2m) part. Then over them lay 6ft (2m) lengths of the $4 \times \frac{1}{4}$in ($10 \times 1$cm) wood, each overlapping the next by $\frac{1}{2}$in (1.5cm), s shown.

(*b*) Place second framing pieces on top of the first ones, andwiching the planks between. Drive thin, oval nails ight through both frame pieces and the intervening planks.

(*c*) Along the whole panel top and bottom, nail more $\times 1\frac{1}{2}$in ($2.5 \times 4$cm) wood to reinforce the otherwise flexible hin planking. Use a heavy hammer or brick in opposition o the hammer strokes.

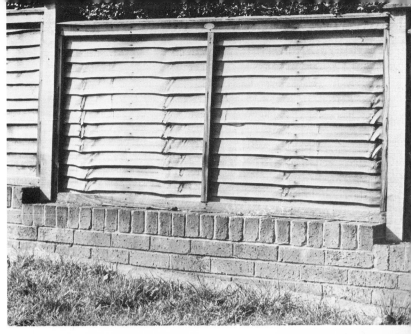

a

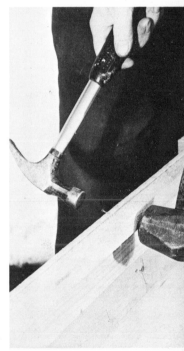

b

c

(*d*) Along the top a broader, $3 \times 1$in ($7.5 \times 2.5$cm), strip an be nailed to protect the edge of the panel from rain.

(*e*) The result is very simple and dignified in appearance nd the panels can be easily screwed or nailed to fence posts. Where panels are used up a slope it is best to make the ends f each slightly diamond-shaped so that the posts are vertical when in position. This is much better in appearance than aving sloping posts.

d

e

3

# PANEL WEAVING

Woven panel fencing is probably the lightest yet toughes[t] peep-proof fencing that can be made at home. The followin[g] tool will take all difficulty out of the job. If you have [a] large fence to make it will save you many hours of labour.

The wood you need for the tool is as follows:

| | |
|---|---|
| Upper and lower beams | Two lengths of 4×2in (10×4cm) wood each 1ft 3in (38cm) longer than th[e] width of panel you wish to make[.] Example: for panels 3ft (1m) wide, th[e] beams should be 4ft 3in (130cm) long[.] |
| Jaw blocks | Made from 2×1in (5×2.5cm) wood you need about 3ft (1m) in all. |
| Uprights | Four lengths of 4×1in (10×2.5cm[)] wood each 8in (20cm) long. |

(*a*) First nail jaw-blocks of wood 3in (8cm) long alon[g] the upper face of the bottom beam, spacing them at width[s] exactly *twice that of the planks you are going to use in you[r] fence*. For example, if your weaving planks are 4in (10cm[)] wide, the spacing between the blocks should be 8in (20cm[)] measured centre to centre (dead accuracy is not vital).

(*b*) At both ends of the bottom beam nail two uprights o[f] 4×1in (10×2.5cm) timber, each 8in (20cm) long, one a[t] each side.

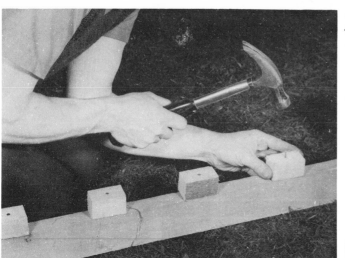

**a** ◀

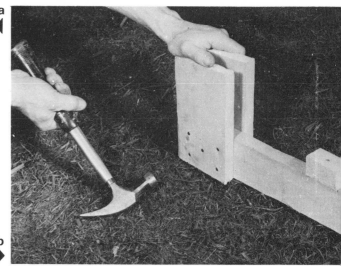

**b** ▶

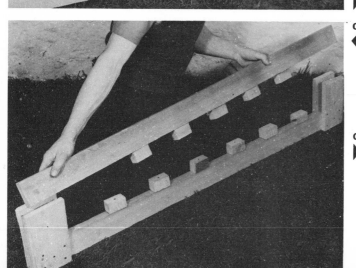

**c** ◀

**d** ▶

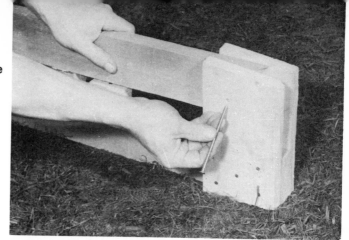

(*c*) Nail similar jaw-blocks to the top beam, but arrange them so that the *block* on the upper beam are opposite the *spaces* between the blocks on the lower beam. Then lower it into the gap between the end supports.

(*d*) Arrange the top and bottom beam so that the blocks are evenly spaced. Then at one end bore right through end supports and upper beam.

(*e*) A heavy nail or bolt through the hole forms a hinge.

## USING THE TOOL

(*f*) Here we show how to use the machine to make panels 6×3ft (2×1m). Take nine weaving planks, each 6ft (2m) long, 4in (10cm) wide and ¼in (1cm) thick. Lay them along the ground, butted edge to edge but *not* overlapping.

(*g*) The end frames of the panels are made from 1in (2.5cm) square timber, 3ft (1m) long, one strip below the ends of the planks, and one strip above. Drive nails down through the end strips and planks to hold them firmly.

(*h*) Lift this end of the panel in your right hand. Draw it through the open jaws of the machine. Lay the panel down on the blocks of the bottom beam, then lower the top one.

(*i*) By moving the panel gently to and fro you can make the blocks on the upper beam push *down* alternate planks whilst the blocks on the lower one push *up* the remainder.

(*j*) With alternate planks held open by the machine it is easy to thread a 3ft (1m) length of plank between them.

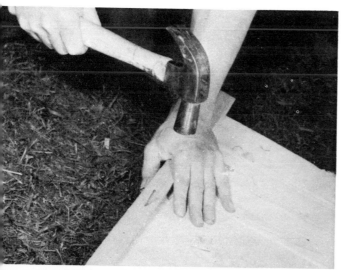

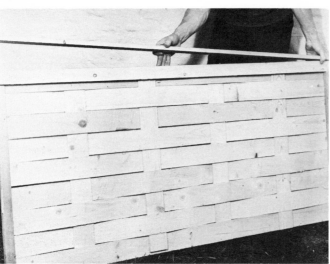

(k) Next pull the panel about 18in (45cm) through the opened jaws. This time, arrange the jaws to push *down* the weaving planks that were raised before and to *lift* the others. Continue in this way to insert further cross strips to form the typical basket-weave pattern. When the end of the panel is reached, this is sandwiched between framing strips exactly as at the beginning (*g*).

(l) It pays also to fasten a framing piece right along the top of the panel, nailing this securely from the rear.

(m) Finally place above it a capping strip of $3 \times \frac{1}{2}$in $(8 \times 1.5$cm) timber.

A panel of this size and type can be made with the machine in about half an hour. With hand weaving only it would take one to two hours and require much more strength and skill.

# AND TAKE CARE WITH THE TOPS OF POSTS

(a) Post tops should *not* be cut off square but rather at an angle. The rain then washes quickly away. This dries the post tops quickly and helps prevent rot.

(b) Better still, nail on a capping of planed timber which will protect further the vulnerable end grain of the post.

A little bitumen paint on top of the posts and even underneath the cappings gives extra protection.

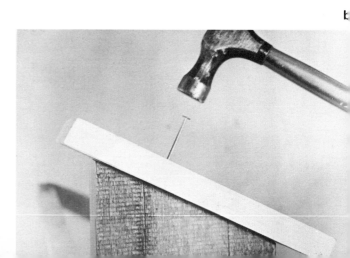

# PALISADE FENCING

## PRACTICALLY BOY- AND PEST-PROOF

Fences made from closely touching poles of timber, erected side by side, are strong, long lasting and require little attention, although fairly expensive to erect. They are also one of the few types of fence that can be set in curves. Palisades give almost complete privacy and (if high enough) are almost impossible to climb.

It is not enough simply to drive these poles into the earth. They must be well secured in a solid concrete foundation. This not only gives the fence stability and strength, but also keep out all sorts of underground creatures—rats, mice, rabbits and so on.

In some places you can buy suitable ready-pointed commercial fence posts, perhaps also pressure-impregnated against rot. Alternatively, you can saw them yourself from peeled rustic pole, pointing their lower ends and treating them well with wood-preservative paint.

## BUT HEAVY WORK

The actual work is simple but does require the mixing of quite a lot of concrete. Since this is heavy labour, do not attempt to do too much at any one time. Four or five yards (metres) of fencing over a weekend is enough for anyone to undertake.

a

b

c

d

(*a*) First dig out a trench, roughly 15in (35cm) wide and deep. Most of the soil removed will be good top soil and can be used to improve the flowerbeds nearby. (Legally speaking, the whole of this trench should be inside your boundary, but your neighbour may agree to arranging the posts down the fence-line.)

(*b*) Stand several posts in line up the centre of the trench and tap their points gently into the ground, just enough to hold them upright. They should just touch each other.

(*c*) As each yard is done, fix the poles together temporarily with laths or waste wood. Nail these to the pole-tops but do not hammer the nails right down. They have to come out again later.

(*d*) Also support the fence against wind with temporary struts of waste pressed into the nearby soil and nailed to the capping. These prevent the fence sagging out of line whilst the concrete is setting.

(*e*) Next, *half*-fill a few yards (metres) of the trench with concrete made from one part cement, three parts of sand and four parts of gravel. Place this both in front and behind the row of poles.

(*f*) Ram it firmly with the end of a pole to get rid of air spaces.

(*g*) It is always best to reinforce the concrete in palisades. Use 1ft (30cm) lengths of thick fencing wire, twisted into hooks at each end.

(*h*) Thrust one end of the wire through the inevitable small gaps between the poles.

(*i*) Then press the ends down into the moist concrete, on both sides of the palisade.

(*j*) Finally fill the trench up completely, so burying the reinforcing wires. Bring the concrete slightly above ground level.

(*k*) Now tap this down to form a 'crown' of cement sloping from the fence, so that rainwater is carried away from the wood.

(*l*) Force the concrete well into the angles between the posts.

(*m*) After at least a week the supporting rails can be removed, but it will take a further three weeks before the concrete has reached full strength, If there is any danger of strong winds leave the supports in longer.

e

# WOODEN WALLS

Railway sleepers or other heavy timber can be used in many ways in gardens, particularly for supporting raised beds or making low retaining walls. A railway sleeper is already well impregnated against rot and requires no further treatment but raw timber must be soaked thoroughly in preservative before use. It is not always necessary to fasten such heavy timbers together, but if it is, the best plan is to bore 1in (2.5cm) diameter holes through any joints and drive in carefully prepared oak pegs. These look well with such heavy material.

The modern timber raised beds illustrated here were constructed for a garden show. The method can be adapted to small private gardens. It is also possible to embed short lengths of railway sleeper vertically, making sure that at least 18in (45cm) is sunk into the soil for every 3ft (1m) of sleeper above.

# TRELLIS AND ESPALIERS

## PAINTING IS IMPORTANT

Wall trellises or frames up which climbing plants can grow are enjoying great popularity at present. There are many kinds, from simple rectangles to complicated diamond trellis. In every case, thorough painting before erection is essential. It is very difficult indeed to remove plants from trellis without injury, or to take a trellis from the wall in order to paint behind it. Some large trellises are deliberately made detachable, which is a good plan where the wall behind is brick and from time to time requires cement pointing. The simplest trellis of all is made by laying $2 \times 1$in ($5 \times 2.5$cm) wood strips in a grille shape, nailing through all the joints. However, in exposed, windy positions these tend to spring apart or flex into diamond pattern. Proper half-lap woodworking joints are better, using quick and easy methods. (See photograph above, page 72 bottom, 73 top.)

## A JOINTED RECTANGULAR FRAME

(*a*) First saw all verticals and cross pieces to length. A useful panel size is $6 \times 3$ft ($2 \times 1$m) but of course this may be varied. Place all the shorter cross pieces together and lay one of the verticals across the bundle. Mark a line on either side of it.

(*b*) Saw down at these points for approximately half the thickness of the cross pieces. Keep the saw-cuts just inside the marks.

a ◀

b ▶

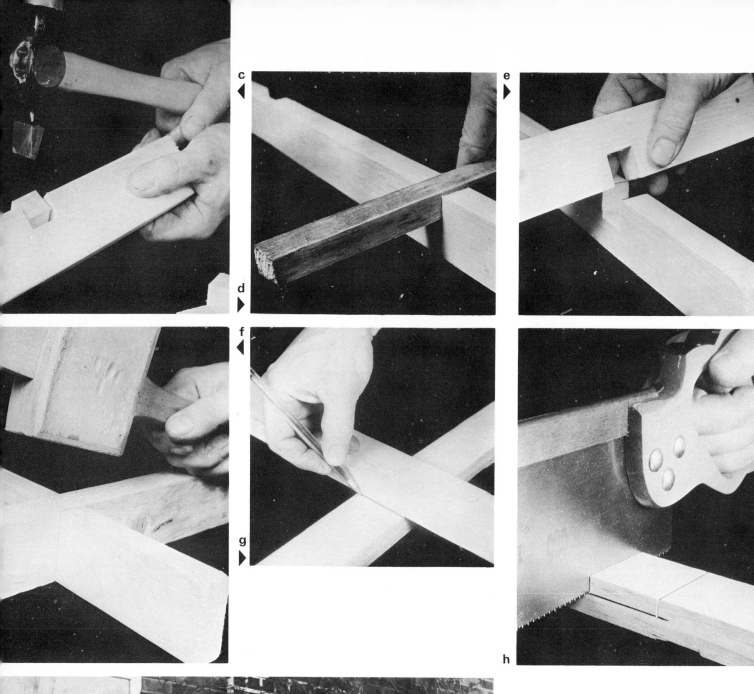

c
d
e
f
g
h

(*c*) One sharp blow from a narrow hammer will knock out the waste, leaving a neat, square joint.

(*d*) Press the verticals down into these joints, where they will usually be a firm fit. Space the verticals and cross pieces to taste, and drive thin nails through the joints.

(*e*) If the uprights and cross pieces are of wood of the same rectangular section make joints in both in the same way so that they slot together . . .

(*f*) . . . and slide solidly to form a first-class cross joint.

(*g*) For flat wood, the 'knock-out' process will not work. Here, overlap the pieces at the joint and mark from both sides of the upper part.

(*h*) Saw down for half the thickness of the timber just inside these marks . . .

(*i*) . . . and pare away the wood between them.

(*j*) This gives two, flat-bottomed joints . . .

(*k*) . . . which will snap together perfectly. Glue, screws or nails can be used to hold the joint solid.

i

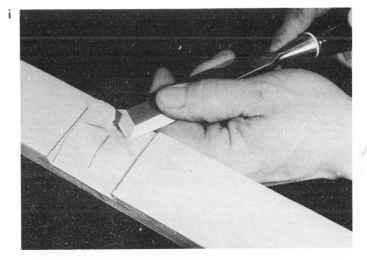

j
◀

k
▶

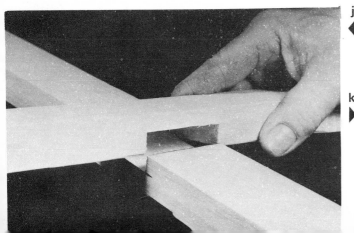

# EXPANDING TRELLIS

You can buy lightweight expanding trellis commercially but it is fairly easy to make your own at home and then you can use rather stronger wood.

The basic idea is simple. Equal lengths of wood 1in (2.5cm) square are nailed together to form a diamond pattern which can be pulled apart or pushed together like a concertina.

## BASED ON AN N-SHAPE

(a) To start you need a large number of strips of wood of exactly equal lengths. The size depends on the width of trellis needed. Wood is usually bought in long lengths. Bind these in bundles, and mark cutting lines across them all. Sawing across the bundle will then produce strips exactly the right size.

(b) The fastenings are 1½in (4cm) round-headed nails.

Take two strips and nail them together 2in (5cm) from the ends, one above the other.

(c) Nail a third strip to the end of one of the first two in similar way, to give an N-shaped pattern.

(d) Take three more strips and place them *between* th outer 'legs' of the N . . .

(e) . . . and grip them between these legs firmly.

(f) The diagonal of the N will now lie across these thre strips. Drive nails down into them through the diagonal, every crossing point.

(g) Add any further number of strips, first under neath . . .

(h) . . . and then on top against the first diagonal.

(i) Drive nails through *all* the joints.

(j) Draw apart the ends and the strips will pivot about th nails and the whole trellis expand in even diamond shape

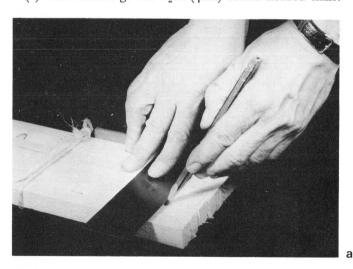

a

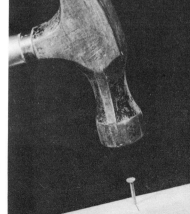

b

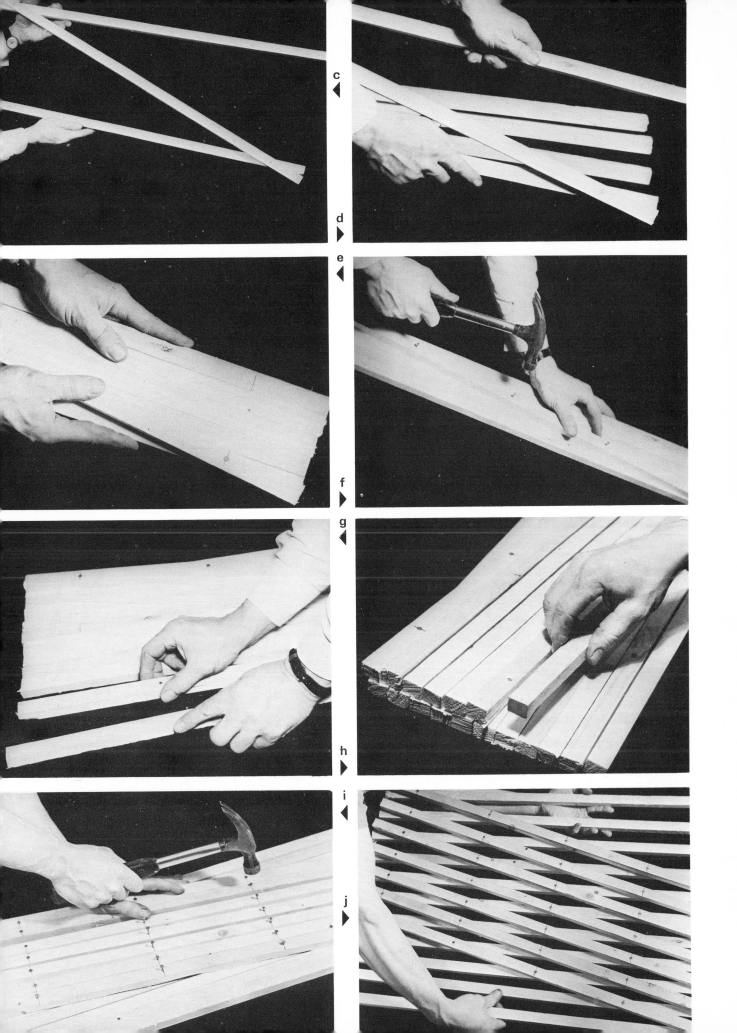

## MAKE IT AS LONG AS YOU WISH

(*k*) By adding further strips underneath . . .

(*l*) . . . and on top you can make trellis as long as you wish.

(*m*) To make a square end you need two shorter strips. The main strips are all long enough to accept *five* nails: now cut two pieces long enough to accept only *three* nails. Place one on top and the other below.

(*n*) You will find that these meet in the middle of t[] trellis instead of at its edges. Nail them through . . .

(*o*) . . . and the trellis end will expand to form a rig[] angle. Such trellises can be fixed direct to simple posts a[] rails.

(*p*) Or by fitting wooden frames around them you c[] make acceptable lightweight fencing panels at a very l[] cost.

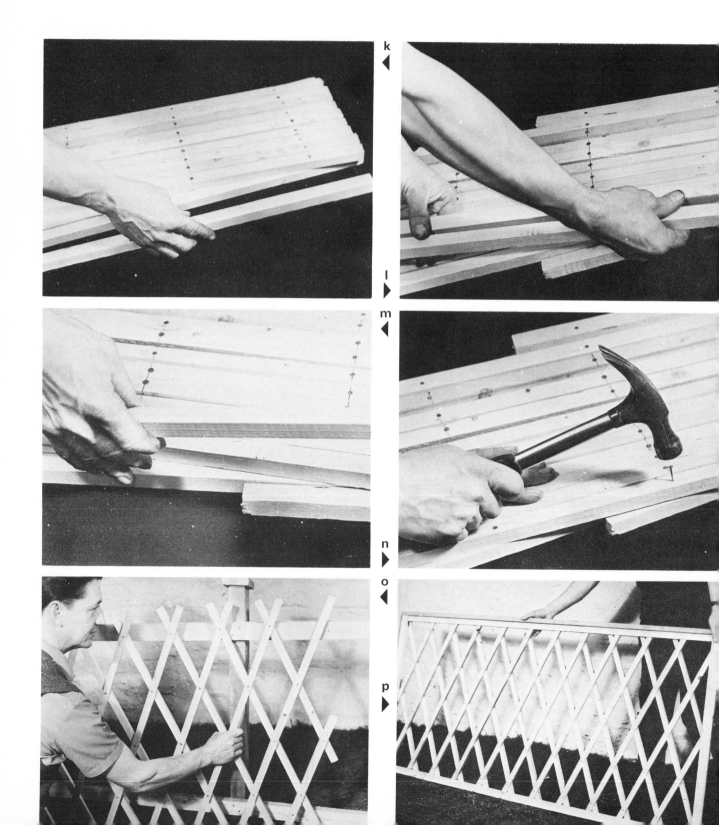

# GARDEN GATES

Few amateurs have to build the gates to their garden. This is usually done by the house builder. However, in course of time a replacement may become necessary, or it may be necessary to make a gate elsewhere in the garden—in fences separating front and rear parts, perhaps, or the flower garden from the vegetables.

All gates are made on much the same principle. The main essential is that a gate should remain rigidly rectangular throughout its life. It must never warp into a diamond shape. With wooden gates this stiffness is given by a diagonal strut, fitted across from corner to corner of the gate frame. No matter what pattern of gate it is, this strut should always form part of it. Metal gates are not usually made at home and those bought commercially are of course designed to be rigid.

Correct erection is also vitally important. The posts must never sag towards each other over the years. This can best be prevented by concreting the bases of *both* posts and joining the concrete together, in one long block (see page 83). No amount of strain then can ever cause the posts to lean inwards, jamming the gate.

There are hundreds of patterns for gates but the two examples shown in the following pages can be developed to give a wide enough choice for most gardens.

# MAKING A RUSTIC GATE

The rustic gate that we show here uses *mitre joints* and illustrates the use of the essential diagonal bracing that must be given to *all* gates.

The size can naturally be varied but should not exceed 4ft in width. Wider gates impose a great strain on the structure, and rustic pole, with its comparatively weak

joints, should not be used for these. Choose sawn, plan timber instead.

### FRAMEWORK

(*a*) The main frame pieces are cut to size, and each end the side pieces cut off at an exact angle of 45°. (See page 1

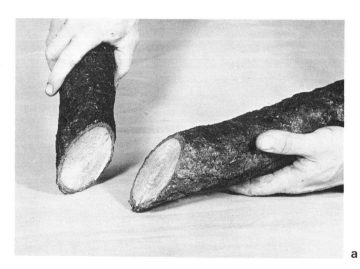

a

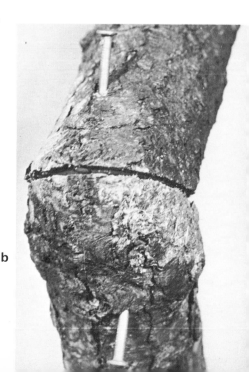

b

for making a tool to help with this.)

(b) The nails are driven diagonally through the corners and offset slightly so as not to strike each other.

(c) Carefully made mitre joints are very neat and strong.

(d) Complete the frame, and try it in position before going on.

## DIAGONAL BRACE

(e) All gates require a diagonal brace to the main frame, otherwise they will rapidly be pushed out of shape. This diagonal is shaped to fit from corner to corner. It is very important that the *lower* end of the diagonal should be placed against the *hinged* side of the gate.

(f) Pare the bark away in the corners of the frame, where the diagonal is to go.

(g) Cut the diagonal to length to give a firm, wood-to-wood fit.

(h) Nail the joint strongly.

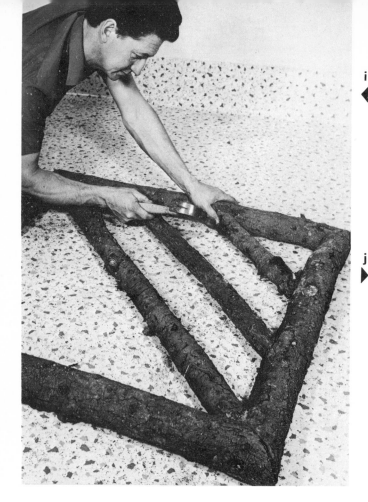

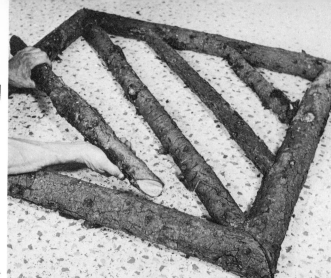

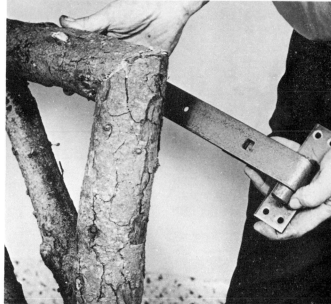

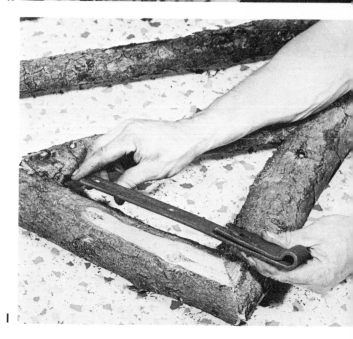

(*i*) The strongest type of rustic gate is made by repeating these diagonals spaced evenly out over the whole gate.

(*j*) Saw the ends of the other diagonals into shallow V-notches to make them bed tightly against the round section of the main frame.

## HINGES

(*k*) Strap-type hinges are essential for garden gates. They may be fitted to the rear of the upper and lower rails. Note again that the hinges *must* be attached at the side of the gate to which the *lower* ends of the diagonals are fitted.

(*l*) Never screw hinges or catches to the *bark* of a rustic gate. Always remove the bark and a small portion of the underlying wood to give a flat solid bed against which the hinges can rest. Otherwise, when the bark flakes away, as it will in due course, the hinges become loose.

A gate made like this can be erected on concrete or wood posts and will keep its shape indefinitely.

# A MODERN FLORAL GATE

Gates made with a box in the top for flowering plants are unusual and charming. You can have a display of flowers and foliage at most seasons. The gate we show here can be adapted to almost any position or size.

### START WITH AN N-SHAPE

(*a*) The key to making a really strong gate is in the basic framework. This is an N-shape, the two uprights being vertical and the diagonal running upwards from the *hinge side* of the gate to the latch side. Start by arranging this N-frame using $5 \times 1\frac{1}{2}$in ($12 \times 4$cm) timber, as shown here. The ends of diagonal are of course sawn off at a suitable angle to make them bed flat against the uprights.

(*b*) Next fit the top and bottom cross members, screwing these firmly into the uprights and the diagonal. Check that the gate is flat and square.

(*c*) Drive more screws from the inside of the diagonal into each of the uprights. This will hold these joints secure.

a

b

c

(*d*) Finally add top and bottom rails at the *back* of the gate in exactly the same way. You will find that this simple square frame with its diagonal brace is very rigid.

## PUT A BASE IN THE BOX

(*e*) Cut a base plank to size and drill several $\frac{3}{4}$in (18mm) holes in it before inserting in the box.

(*f*) Nails driven in through the cross rails hold the base of the plant box.

## PLANK PATTERN AND HINGES

(*g*) On the basic frame any patterning of planks can be fixed, vertical or horizontal, closely butted to give a solid gate or spaced apart to give a lighter effect.

It is very important to fix the hinges on the correct side of the gate. They must always be screwed at the side which has the *bottom* end of the diagonal or the gate will sag.

(*h*) For maximum strength pass two bolts clean through the largest hinge hole and the whole thickness of the gate. Ordinary woodscrews will serve in the smaller holes.

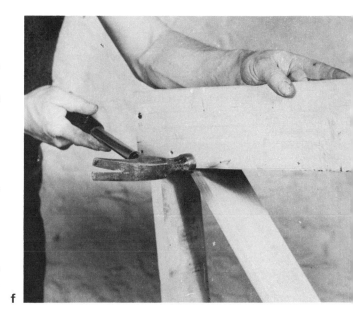

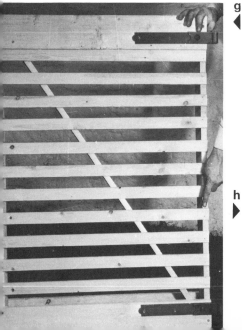

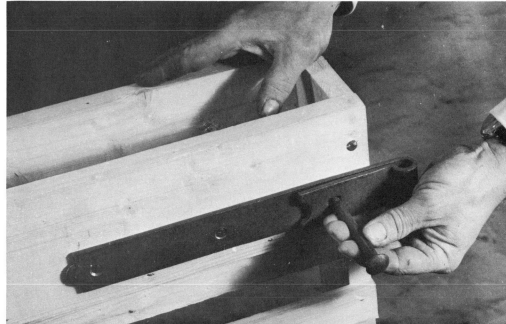

# ERECTING GATES

A garden gate that sags soon becomes difficult to open. The problem is often caused by the posts sinking inwards towards each other. It is essential to give gate-posts really secure foundations, to fix them the correct distance apart, and to prevent them tilting inwards later.

## THE TRENCH

(a) Setting the posts deeply in concrete is the only certain way to success. This concrete should be in the form of one solid block across the full width of the gateway. First, dig out a trench 12in (30cm) wide across the whole width from post to post.

(b) At the two ends where the posts will stand the depth of the trench must be at least 18in (45cm), but across the centre, below the gate, 9in (23cm) is enough.

## LOWER GATE AND POSTS IN ONE OPERATION

(c) Next, assemble the gate and both its posts, including hinges but not catches. Posts should be embedded to a depth of roughly 18in, or one-third of the gate's height, whichever is the greater.

(d) Hold gate and posts together with temporary struts nailed across from post to post.

(e) Place one or two shovels of concrete (mixed in proportions of one part cement, two parts of sand and three parts of gravel) on the bottoms of the trench ends.

(f) Lower the gate on its posts into the trench.

83

(*g*) Fill up the entire trench to the brim. Ram the concrete well as you fill, to make sure that all air spaces are forced out.

## TEMPORARY SUPPORT

(*h*) If the gate is in a windy position, support it by temporary struts so that there will be no movement until the concrete has set. This takes a few days with ordinary cement, but you can add chemicals which speed up drying to only a few hours.

(*i*) For a final improvement support both posts by diagonal struts carefully sawn and nailed to their outer faces.

(*j*) Once the concrete is completely set remove the temporary struts. The gate will now stand securely for many years.

(*k*) You will find that by this method of erection the gate fits very closely to its post, enabling catches to be neatly and easily fitted.

# GARDEN WALLS

### BUILD LOW FOR SAFETY

Garden walls can be built to screen part of the garden, to retain soil on slopes, or simply for decoration. Each kind of wall has its own special problems.

A *screen wall* must usually be tall, which for amateur work limits the choice of materials. Only lightweight concrete screenblocks can safely be built up to more than 4ft (120cm).

A *retaining wall* supporting soil is even more difficult, unless it is no more than 18in (45cm) high. The pressure behind such walls is very great—several tons per square yard in clay areas—so only the strongest of structures will do. Low banks can best be held up by a rock-garden construction (see pages 106–8).

Fortunately most garden walls are built for decoration and these present fewer difficulties. You can safely build walls up to 3ft (1m) high in any normal material such as stone, concrete blocks or brick. The methods used are similar in each case. The drystone planted wall is the easiest of all and certainly very attractive. Cemented stone is not too difficult, and you should have no trouble with concrete blocks or bricks.

Within these limits you can feel confident even if you have never touched a trowel or mixed mortar before.

## FIRST CHOOSE YOUR MATERIAL

Wall material is expensive. Ready-shaped stone can cost several pounds per square yard. Concrete blocks are cheaper and bricks, if bought secondhand, cost still less. Screen-blocks are not expensive either, and you can even make these yourself, though it does take some time (see pages 118–22).

For easy reference we give below the pros and cons of each material. Methods of construction in each are given in detail in subsequent main sections.

### Drystone walls

In their simplest form these are walls built of flat stones (sometimes broken concrete slabs), with soil instead of mortar in the joints. This makes them easy to build or alter later. Plants can be grown on them and they eventually become a striking feature in the garden. The true drystone wall, without *any* jointing material, should only be tackled after some practice with the soil-bonded type. For either kind use sandstone or limestone, which split flat naturally and are easy to handle, besides being comparatively cheap since the stone is bought untrimmed, straight from the quarry. The suppliers will advise what weight of their particular stone you need per square yard of wall.

## Cemented stone

This can be the most expensive of all wall materials if professionally prepared square blocks are used, but it is quite possible to build attractive garden walls using only rough quarried stone, and doing the shaping yourself in the garden (see page 95). A few irregularities do not matter—indeed they add to the charm of the wall. You can build cemented stone blocks up to 3ft (1m) high provided they are also relatively thick. Again, the suppliers will advise on quantities.

## Screenblocks

These lightweight openwork concrete blocks can be built up to 6ft (2m) without risk, provided that their pillars are properly reinforced. There are many different types of block, but all tend to be rather fragile. Breakages are likely, so always order one or two extra. The cost per square yard is moderate. Bricks or concrete blocks combine well with screenblocks to give 'mixed' walls that are economical and swiftly built. Screenblock walls take less working time to erect than any other type.

## Concrete blocks

Precast concrete blocks are sold in many shapes and sizes. They can also be made at home. All are easy to build, requiring practically no skill, but they are not cheap. Limit the height to 3ft (1m) for blocks up to 4in (10cm) wide; 4ft (120cm) for blocks 9in (23cm) wide. How you order depends on the maker, who will often supply blocks ready to build up to a specific pattern.

## Bricks

New bricks are *not* usually attractive in a garden but you can often buy weathered second-hand bricks which have attained a pleasing colour over the years. These are easy to build, being regular in shape, and are fairly cheap. Mortar is always used. Limit the height to 3ft (1m) for walls one brick thick; 4ft (120cm) for a double thickness, provided you take care to build truly vertical. Order fifty bricks for every square yard of single-brick wall.

# BUILDING A DRYSTONE
# PLANTED WALL

Building low decorative walls without cement is one of the easier garden construction jobs. These walls can be very attractive when clothed in flowers and creepers. Try to fit them into your garden plan in some unexpected way. This wall, for example, can be used as a *seat*.

Almost any type of flat stone can be used, the easiest being slabs of sandstone or limestone. Wide, flat stones are much easier to build with than thick or irregularly shaped kinds. You can even build with broken *concrete* slabs (with the broken edges outwards).

## FOUNDATIONS

(*a*) Unlike most kinds of wall, these decorative drystone structures do not require deep or concrete foundations. It is enough as a rule to dig out the soil for a depth of 6–8in (15–20cm), but obviously, much depends on the type of ground in your garden. You must go deeper, for example, in soft sand.

(*b*) When you have taken out the appropriate depth, tread the subsoil firm and hard.

## THE RIGHT TAPER

(c) All drystone walls must be built thinner at the top than at the bottom, by about one-fifth. This is easy if you make a pair of wooden guides lightly nailed together.

(d) Drive these into the ground at each end of your wall. As you build, check the slopes by sighting along them.

(e) Choose the thickest stones for the base and arrange them with their best edges facing outwards. It helps to hammer the soil underneath them with a long-nosed hammer.

(f) Complete the first row, front and back, in this way. Each stone must slope slightly inwards to make the rain drain into the wall rather than off it. Check this by laying a strip of wood across the rows of stone.

(g) Spread a ½in (12mm) layer of fine soil over the stones.

(h) Then press the next row of stones, front and back, over the first, and still tilting slightly inwards. Continue upwards in this way, spreading soil and adding layers of stone. Stagger the joints as for bricks in a wall.

(*i*) Fill the gaps between, in every layer, with the smaller stones. Trim any awkwardly shaped pieces with a hammer and chisel or the back of a mason's hammer.

(*j*) As the wall rises check that it is tapering accurately by sighting along the wooden guides, and by stretching strings between them. Add small creeping plants in the soil-beds as the wall is built.

### THE CAPPING

(*k*) For the final capping of this wall use large rectangular slabs of thin sandstone. These make excellent seats, but take care in lifting them. It is best to get help if you can. Check that the tops are either dead level or sloping very slightly to the rear.

(*l*) The gaps between the seat slabs can also be filled with plants. (Indeed, if you wish, the *whole* top of the wall can be left open and planted.)

(*m*) Walls of this kind blend with most informal gardens and, except for watering the plants, require practically no attention and will last for many years.

# THE TRUE DRYSTONE WALL

The true drystone wall is built without any jointing material whatever (though mortar can be used for the capping). The stone blocks are held together purely by their close fit and small wedges of natural stone. Flat blocks of sandstone and limestone are again the most suitable. Building follows the lines of the soil-bonded type. The cost depends on available local stones, to be ordered by weight. Partly dressed stone costs more, and is bought not by weight but by *area*. Make sure that the wall faces taper uniformly (page 89). Each stone should be laid tilted *very slightly* inwards, towards the wall centre, for stability.

(*a*) Most stones in each row should be of roughly the same size. This makes for speed and ease of building. Occasionally though, insert single large blocks rising through two courses or more. This improves the look of the wall. Long slabs stretching right through the thickness of the wall are also used at intervals to hold its two faces firmly together.

(*b*) The top may be left 'dry' but is usually reinforced. Here vertically placed stones are bedded firmly into mortar. This locks the upper part of the wall solidly together and also prevents rain from entering and weakening the structure.

Remember that the 3ft (1m) limit of height for amateur work should never be exceeded.

a ◀

b ▶

# CEMENTED STONE WALLS

Natural stone, the most attractive of all garden wall materials, is the most expensive when bought dressed and shaped, but a good cemented wall can be built with much cheaper stone straight from the quarry. Sandstones and limestones split naturally into blocks that are roughly flat at top and bottom, making them easier to build with. The thickness of individual blocks in your load will vary, so the first job is to sort the stones into groups of roughly equal thickness. This not only saves time when building but ensures the best use of materials.

Amateurs should not build such walls higher than 3ft (1m); heavy stone collapsing from that sort of height has a dangerous momentum.

## SOLID FOUNDATIONS

It is essential to give all cemented stone walls solid foundations to support their weight and prevent subsidence. Dig out the soil until a firm base is reached. In heavy land this may be only 6in (15cm) deep, but in light sand 12in (30cm) will not be too much. Foundations are shallowest on hard-packed gravelly soil. All foundations must be broader than the walls they support, at least double the thickness, and more in light soils.

(a) Whatever the depths of the foundation trench, fill it to within 2in (5cm) of the soil surface with well-rammed broken bricks and stone rubble. Then on top of this spread a 3–4in (7.5–10cm) layer of concrete as a foundation for the actual building.

(b) After this first layer of mortar has dried spread a further layer about $\frac{1}{2}$in (1.5cm) deep on which the stones themselves can be bedded.

## BUILDING UP

(c) Choose large blocks of stone for the base of the wall and tap them gently down into the still-moist mortar. Leave a gap of roughly $\frac{1}{4}$in (6mm) between the stones.

a ◄

b ►

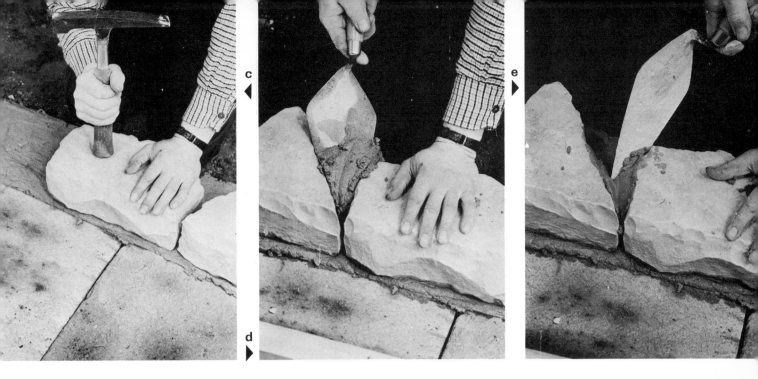

(d) Then, working from the rear, squeeze more mortar between the stones.

(e) Press this tightly against the stones on either side, using the tip of the trowel. Where the rear of the wall will *not* be visible, as in retaining walls, you can use broken rubble or brick-ends to fill up any gaps behind and between the stones.

(f) Scoop away any surplus mortar that squeezes out from below the base of the stones.

(g) Use a spirit-level (rested on a much longer board) to check that the first course is reasonably flat.

(h) Spread more cement over the tops of the first row of stones, keeping it away from the front face of the wall.

(i) Now press a second row of stones into this mortar. Make sure that the joints are 'staggered'; that is, that the joints between the second row of stones are *not* directly above the joints of the lower row.

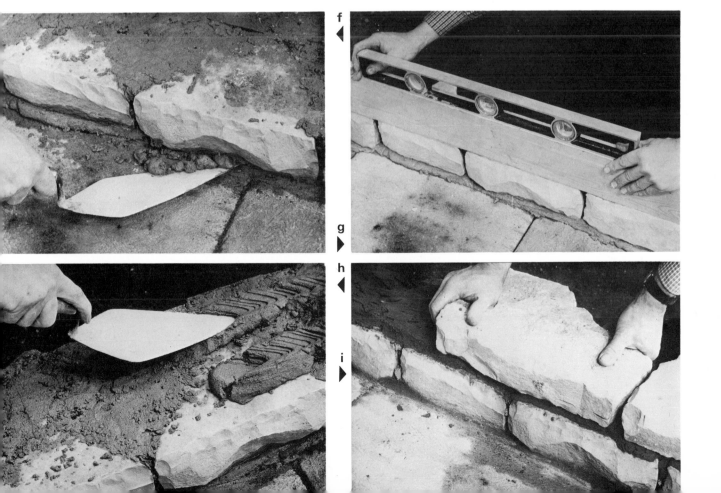

(j) Walls visible from both sides must have good stone on both faces. However, one is often less important than the other, and here smaller pieces can be used. Squeeze plenty of mortar between such small stones to hold them securely.

## FINISHING OFF

(k) The top of the wall can be made in a variety of ways. The simplest is to save broad, large slabs and fit them together to extend like a capping from the front to back of the wall.

(l) Allow the wall to set for twenty-four hours. Then use the tip of a pick, or even a screwdriver blade, to rake out the joint mortar $\frac{1}{4}$in (6mm) deep. Fill these up neatly with a fine mortar, perhaps in a contrasting colour. A small trowel will be needed for this.

(m) After this mortar has partly dried (usually the following day), a brisk brushing will remove surplus lumps and leave the stone neat.

As with most natural stone, a skilful blending of occasional large pieces with thinner ones makes a great deal of difference to the final appearance (see photograph at top of page 95 and the professionally finished wall shown below).

# SHAPING STONE BLOCKS FOR WALLS

Although garden walling stone, especially sandstone and
limestone, may be delivered practically ready to use, it is
often necessary to finally trim the blocks to shape. Although
top-class masonry work is very highly skilled, most amateurs
can safely attempt this sort of job. A mason's chisel, a
hammer and a pair of cheap goggles (to protect the eyes from
flying chips) are all the tools needed.

Shaping blocks for wall building involves choosing one
side as the 'face', or outward-looking side, and shaping the
rest of the block to fit. Usually, one face will already be
fairly flat, and without major blemishes. For best results
the 'grain' of the stone should be horizontal.

(*a*) First, mark the line right round all four sides of the
face', about ½in (1.2cm) back from it.

(*b*) With the block face turned *away* from you, chisel the
stone outwards from the line you have drawn, to leave the
centre of the face rather higher than its edges. This is a
traditional method of dressing stone blocks for garden use.
This raised face *can* be cut flat by taking off further chips,
but this is a long operation and not usually necessary.

(*c*) Then, if required, shape the two ends of the block by
marking and chiselling them in the same way, at right
angles to the face.

(*d*) The result will be a square-ended block with a raised
face, which can be built into very pleasing garden walls.

a

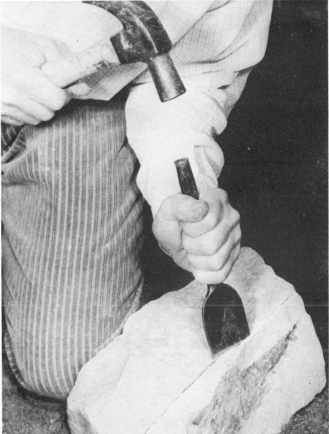

b

c ◀

d ▶

# BUILDING WALLS WITH SCREENBLOCKS

Screenblocks, or decorative castings in various openwo[rk] patterns, are the only type of wall material that can be safe[ly] built up to 6ft by an amateur. They are usually light[weight] weight, so low walls do not require deep foundation[s]. However, a dead-level base *is* required, so at the very lea[st] give a few inches of concrete.

There are many patterns of screenblock available, som[e] square and others rectangular. Naturally, the thinner th[e] sections of the particular pattern, the more fragile th[e] block will be. However, since garden walls of this type a[re] not designed to bear loads this is not important.

The quality of the casting may be judged to some exte[nt] by the texture of the concrete. An open, porous surfac[e] usually indicates a weaker block than one presenting a fin[e] smooth surface. Another test of quality is to measu[re] accurately the length and width of several blocks. Goo[d] castings do not vary but in the cheaper sorts there may b[e] differences. This naturally makes for slightly more difficu[lt] building.

There is a wide variation in cost between the cheapest an[d] most expensive types. These last are really intended for us[e] in high-quality buildings and are made to a much highe[r] standard of texture, finish and strength than is needed f[or] an ordinary garden wall. Blocks are made in brown[s,] whites and greys; there are also reds, blues and yellows, bu[t] these more exotic colours should be used with great cautio[n.] Appearance, availability and price are the key factors i[n] deciding which type to buy.

Long screenblock walls should be supported at interva[ls] of 6–8ft (2–2.5m) by pillars. Many firms supply special[ly] moulded pillar blocks which accept the edges of the scree[n] blocks in side slots. Such pillars are often hollow and th[e] open centre is then filled with fine concrete round a ste[el]

**a**

**b**

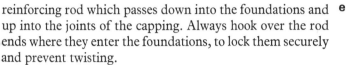

reinforcing rod which passes down into the foundations and up into the joints of the capping. Always hook over the rod ends where they enter the foundations, to lock them securely and prevent twisting.

## A DEAD-LEVEL BASE

(a) Take out a trench at least twice as wide as the wall's thickness down to firm subsoil.

(b) Break into this all types of stone and brick rubble, well rammed together.

(c) Finally top this with at least 3in (7.5cm) of well-mixed concrete. Chop it down into the rubble . . .

(d) . . . and smooth it off level with a length of timber.

(e) Check it for exact level, both along and across the concrete. On such a base, left for a week to set, building will be quick and easy.

## ACCURACY IS IMPORTANT

(f) For accurate building, always start by stretching guidestrings along front and rear of the wall, a block's thickness apart.

(*g*) Begin building by spreading a small roll of mortar along the surface of your foundation and spread this out along the length where the first few blocks are to rest. The 'foundation' shown here consists of heavy solid blocks. Screenblocks can also be set on existing walls, to raise their height or improve their appearance.

(*h*) Lower the screenblock gently into place and press it down. Hand pressure should be enough, but if anything more is needed, use a small block of wood; never hammer it down with a *metal* tool. In spite of their apparent strength these concrete blocks are rather fragile.

(*i*) Check for level vertically . . .

(*j*) . . . and horizontally. This is very important. Errors in alignment may cause the finished wall to collapse.

(*k*) Mortar the side-end of the next block.

(*l*) Slide the blocks gently together. Make the finished

mortar joint roughly $\frac{3}{8}$in (1cm) thick. Draw away any squeezed-out mortar with the tip of the trowel.

## REINFORCING THE JOINTS FOR A TALL WALL

(*m*) For walls taller than approximately 3ft (1m), it is best to reinforce the joints with soft iron rods, obtainable from building merchants. These rods can be easily bent over at the tips with a long pair of pincers.

(*n*) These hook-ended rods are laid through horizontal and vertical joints . . .

(*o*) . . . so that they can be buried in the mortar. For a high wall of this type, the vertical joints between blocks must be directly above each other. However, when there is no need to reinforce joints, blocks are fitted together with the vertical joints *not* aligned one above the other but bonded.

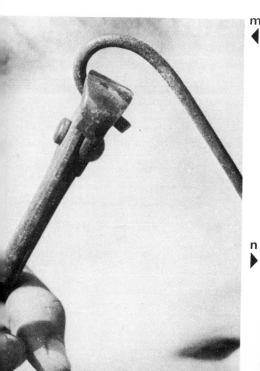

## BONDING

(*p*) To get this correct bonding start with a *half-length* block on the second row.

(*q*) Press the 'half' gently into place and check for horizontal and vertical alignment.

(*r*) Spread the mortar for the next **few** blocks. Do not use too much. Remove any surplus overhanging the edges before water is squeezed out down the faces of the blocks below.

(*s*) Continue building to the required height, starting with a half block on alternate rows. Cover new cement work to protect it from either heavy rain or hot sun. Damp sacking is best, but black polythene sheet will serve.

# BUILDING IN BRICKS AND BLOCKS

You can only become a bricklayer by laying bricks. Here we show the simplest way to start—on a wall one brick or block thick and not very high.

## SOLID FOUNDATIONS SPREAD THE LOAD

There is no difference between building with housebricks or the many kinds of precast decorative wall blocks. For all of them a good foundation is essential to ensure that the weight of the wall is carried by solid ground and not by soft top soil. The concrete foundation also spreads the load of the narrow brick over a wider area: it should be at least double, preferably three times, the thickness of the bricks.

The exact *depth* to dig to depends on the height of the wall and the kind of soil. Deep foundations are needed in clay because it expands and contracts over the years. In sand too, deep foundations are necessary. Medium-heavy soil does not need quite as much depth for garden walls, but even so go down several inches until you reach solid subsoil, as shown on page 97 for screenblock walling.

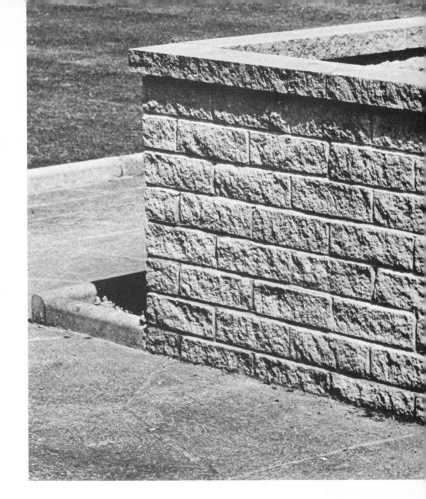

## ALIGN AND CHECK CONTINUALLY

(*a*) Before starting to build, fix two lines a brick's-width apart along the whole length of the foundation. Mix a mortar of one part cement to four parts of soft sand, adding just enough water to make it workable but not too wet. A mixed in 'plasticiser' is also helpful; this is a chemical which makes the mortar easier to spread. Scoop up a small roll of mortar and lay it neatly on the foundation between the lines. Skilled bricklayers use larger trowels than the one shown here, which spread the mortar further at a stroke.

(*b*) Draw the lines apart and place your first brick carefully between them on top of the mortar. Squeeze the brick down, using moderate hand pressure. If it is very stiff to press down, then the mortar may be too dry. It more often happens that mortar mixed by an amateur is too *soft* and loses water under pressure. In this case, remix your mortar, adding more dry-mixed material, to a stiffer consistency.

(*c*) Check this first brick with a spirit-level to see that it is flat.

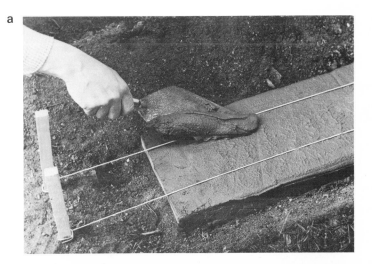

a

b

c

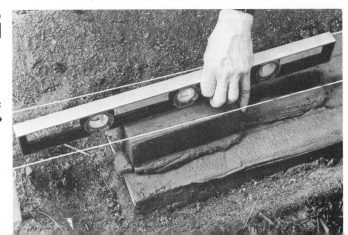

(d) Then give it a final tap with the *wooden* part of a tool to straighten it.

(e) Lay a second brick crossways on top of the first, the guide strings passing beneath it at either side.

(f) Slide the strings up the pegs so that they are drawn taut beneath the upper brick and exactly aligned with the corners of the lower brick. Repeat the whole operation at the other end of your wall.

(g) Next take up half a trowel of mortar and hold it above the end of the next brick. Sweep the trowel down and backwards, to draw half the mortar onto the brick end.

(h) Then shift the trowel to the other side of the brick and sweep *forwards* to draw off the remaining half.

(i) This will leave two mortar blobs as shown here.

(j) Squeeze the brick end up against its neighbour.

(k) Cut away surplus mortar from beneath the brick with the edge of the trowel . . .

(l) . . . and smooth off the top where it has squeezed up between the two bricks.

## BUILD THE ENDS FIRST

(m) Lay four or five bricks at each end of the wall. Then place a mortar bed for a second row on top of them. To start this second row you need a half-brick, which you can easily cut by laying a broad chisel across a whole brick and striking it a sharp blow with a heavy hammer. Press the half-brick into the mortar. This half-brick ensures that the joints between the bricks will not come directly above each other in succeeding rows, so greatly strengthening the wall.

(n) Cut away at once any squeezed-out mortar or it may mark the wall face. Water running down indicates a too-wet mortar. Sandy mortar that will not stick may be too dry.

(o) Raise the lines again but this time trap them below the cross brick close against the corners of the brick beneath. Alternatively, cement in a third brick, and tie the strings to nails pushed into the mortar joint.

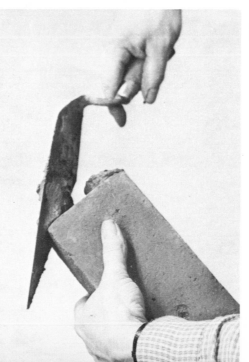

p

(*p*) Check the completed rows for level. (The strings have been removed for clarity in this and subsequent photos.)

(*q*) Build upwards at both the wall *ends*, reducing the number of bricks on each row, and checking to make sure that the ends of the walls are rising vertically.

(*r*) After building a section draw the trowel tip up the vertical joints . . .

(*s*) . . . and then along the horizontal joints. Press the upper edge of the trowel a little beneath the lower edge of the upper bricks to squeeze the mortar inwards to a slight slope. This keeps rain out of the joints.

(*t*) Finally brush away surplus, half-dried cement from the face of the bricks.

(*u*) Build both ends of the wall to full height before filling in between them. Irregularities show up most at the ends. Also, the completed brick rows can now be used to carry more guide-strings, so keeping the rows level right along the wall.

## FILLING IN

(*v*) However, continue to check the levels with boards as the ends are built out to meet each other.

(*w*) At the last brick of all, mortar the ends of the laid bricks . . .

(*x*) . . . and press the last brick between, working from the front of the wall. Remember always to cover new brickwork if there is any chance of frost or in very hot, dry weather.

q

r
s

t
u
v

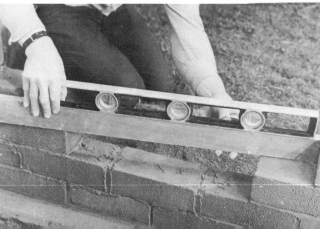

# COMBINATION WALLS

Many materials are used for building walls but it is not always easy to combine them together. Indeed, landscape architects argue heatedly about whether you can *ever* blend concrete with stone or stone with brick.

However, mixing brick and concrete together is fairly well accepted, as in this garden wall which uses bricks and lightweight concrete screenblocks. These, in combination with brick, can be used in low walls and screens between one part of the garden and another or on garden boundaries. They should not be built taller than about 4ft (1m). The base wall is built exactly as shown on pages 101–5.

(*a*) Then, on the side of the screenblock being laid, spread two thin parallel strips of mortar.

(*b*) Press this mortared side up to the neighbouring block, and down onto a mortar bed. Draw the trowel tip up between the two blocks to clean out the joint.

(*c*) Add a brick layer on top of the screenblocks, followed by a concrete capping. Various other patterns can be easily worked out.

a

b
▶

c

# BUILDING A ROCK GARDEN

### THE IDEAL

A rock garden can be built as a feature in its own right, or perhaps as part of the surroundings of a pool. It can be just a few feet across or as large as you wish. But it must look as nearly as possible like a natural outcrop of rock. Avoid the spotted-dog or currant-bun effect.

Rocks in nature lie in strata; long, flat blocks of much the same thickness. Occasional crags may burst through these, forming peaks, gorges and cliffs. These same features are modelled in miniature when building a rock garden.

This job calls for energy and an artistic eye. Since the rock itself will weigh perhaps several tons, and each individual piece must be buried in the soil, it is *not* a job to be hurried through in a few spare hours!

*but how do you get it on-site?*

A true alpine garden needs sun. Alpine plants must have well-drained soil and plenty of light. Few rock gardens d well if overhung by trees. This is due not so much to th shade as to the falling leaves in autumn, which lie over th plants and kill them. Many alpines also like to have lime i the soil, or to grow over limestone rocks.

Ideally, stone for rock gardens should not be raw blaste rock from the quarry but stones that have lain on the surfac exposed to the weather for many years. They should b pleasing in colour, richly worn and textured, and perhap covered with moss and lichen. (Try to preserve these plant when the rock garden is being built.)

## HARD WORK

(a) Start at the foot of the rockery bank by excavating a trench along the line of what is to be the lowest row of stones.

(b) Press large stones down into the trench, keeping their best faces forward and arranging them as naturally as possible, in somewhat irregular curves.

(c) Pull down soil to fill up behind the first row. This produces a 'shelf' in the soil above, into which you can press more stones. Most stones have a natural 'grain', which as a rule, should be kept horizontal.

(d) Use large and small pieces, aiming always to attain a natural appearance. Work fine soil into and over the joints so that the stones look like protruding pieces of much larger rocks buried below the soil.

(e) Avoid too regular an appearance. Place groups of rocks slightly apart. The boundary of a rock garden may be defined with rows of stones or its plants can be allowed to grow outward irregularly.

## REWARDS

(*f*) Groups of large stones built up on each other can make impressive cliffs. Plants can be inserted here in soil between the blocks . . .

(*g*) . . . and will soon develop and soften the harsh edges of the fresh rocks.

(*h*) Cushions of rapid-growing plants give a natural established appearance.

(*i*) Miniature rock groups, perhaps with tiny trees, can be set in lawns and require little maintenance.

(*j*) Low rockeries can also be used as retaining banks between differing levels of the garden. Make sure that they slope backwards at least 45° or the pressure of soil behind may push them over.

# MIXING CEMENT AND CONCRETE

Nothing is more important in building than careful mixing of mortar and concrete. All too often this side of the work is neglected. The results are weak walls, mortar that flakes to pieces in frost, cast blocks that crumble and crack. The commonest mistake is to use too much water. Another is to mix too much at one time. Hand mixing is laborious therefore mix only in small quantities. Hire a power mixer if you have much to do.

## THE RIGHT METHOD

(a) First mix all the materials together *dry*. Pile them to-

gether and then shovel them completely aside to make a second heap. Then shovel *this* pile back again and repeat the operation five times. The result will be an evenly-coloured mix. For **mortar,** next open out a hole in the heap top.

(b) Pour water into the hole but not adding much at any one time . . .

(c) . . . turn the mix into the water from the sides of the pile. Continue till the whole mix is evenly moist and stiff.

(d) Well-mixed mortar should support the shovel and should not lose water onto the working surface.

When mixing **concrete,** do not open up a hole for water in the top of the pile, but sprinkle the water over from a fine-rosed watering can, turning it till it is evenly moist.

## THE RIGHT MIX

In mortar and concrete mixing, all measurements are by volume, not weight.

The **basic mortar mix** is three parts of soft sand to one part of cement; a four to one mix can be used where strength is less important. For block casting, use concreting sand, which is sharper and coarser.

All **concretes** include gravel as well as sand and cement, in various proportions (these are given in the text at the sections concerned).

**Waterproof concretes** for ponds are made by using a ready waterproofed cement or adding waterproofing agents as the mixing is done. It is most important to follow the instructions given by the manufacturers.

**Extra rapid drying cements** or special additives are available where speed is vital but they are more expensive and the results may not be quite so strong. Never buy cement to keep in stock. Always purchase it as needed. It absorbs moisture even through a sealed bag and becomes useless within a few months.

# MAKING YOUR OWN BUILDING MATERIALS

## TAKE SAND, CEMENT AND WOOD

It is not difficult to make your own building blocks and paving slabs, and the saving is quite large. In fact the cost of sand and cement may be only a quarter the price of commercially produced blocks.

Nor do you need very complicated equipment, You can make satisfactory casting using little more than a few planks of wood, temporarily nailed together as moulds.

Although blocks can be made individually it is naturally quicker and easier to make a group of six or eight at the same time. The sizes may not turn out exact but this is of little importance in garden work.

The concrete used is a mixture of one part of cement to three parts of concrete sand. Mix these together *dry*, and then add water to form a mixture which is *damp* rather than wet. On no account make it soft and sloppy. Thorough mixing makes all the difference to the quality of the blocks.

Some block types cannot be 'mass produced' and for these individual moulds are needed.

*Top left:* home-cast building blocks

*Bottom left:* paving slabs

*Centre:* screenblocks are more difficult, but some design can be made at home

*Right:* circular slab, with a pebble-textured surface

## AND CAST WALL BLOCKS

(a) Any level surface will do for the job—even flat-raked soil or a lawn. Spread a sheet of polythene (cheaply purchased from any builders' supply merchants) over the surface.

(b) For moulds you need planks whose width is equal to the thickness of block that you wish to make. Here we show wood about 5in (roughly 13cm) wide. Stand four planks on edge, in a conveniently sized rectangle.

(c) Support the corners with bricks placed on the outside of the framework. Also drive thin nails through the corners to secure them more firmly, but do *not* make the structure too rigid. It has to be knocked apart later.

(d) Spread the concrete mixture within your mould.

(e) Work it well down, using a chopping action with a spade to get rid of air holes. See that the edges and corners are completely filled.

(f) Beat a length of wood across the surface to flatten the concrete level with the edges of your mould.

**g** ◀

**h** ▶

**i** ◀

**j** ▶

(*g*) Smooth the surface with a trowel and leave it to set for about an hour. (The exact time varies, less in warm conditions, more when it is cold, but it is not critical anyway.)

(*h*) Then, when the surface 'crust' has formed, use straight-edge and the edge of a trowel to slice the still-moist concrete into rectangles. Do not cut completely through but just one-third of its thickness. The edge of a trowel will do as a tool.

(*i*) Allow the blocks now to set for a further twenty-four hours. Then remove the supporting bricks and tap away the mould. This should come cleanly away at all sides.

(*j*) Slide a spade under the edge to lift the block, which will probably split across at one or other of its markings.

(*k*) To break the blocks completely, place a short length of thin timber directly underneath one slit and press down on both sides until the block parts cleanly.

**k**

(*l*) The faces made by breaking are rough and will often serve well without further trimming. However, you can also trim the block to some extent by using a steel shaping tool. The blocks must now be left to 'cure'. They will not reach full strength for four weeks. Stack them under light cover so that air can pass around and between them all. Protection from frost is vital.

**l**

# PAVING SLAB CASTING

Slabs for paving can be cast in a similar manner to building blocks, except that the moulds are shallower. Arrange moulding boards 3 × 1in (7.5 × 2.5cm) in section to surround a flat area roughly 6 × 3ft (2 × 1m). Support the corners with pegs. Spread within it a layer of sand, roughly 1in (2.5cm) thick. Then mix a mortar of one part cement to three parts of concreting sand.

(*a*) Spread the mortar within the mould and beat it down level with the top of the boards. Aim for a slab thickness of about 2in (5cm).

(*b*) After four hours the mortar will have begun to set. Use a straight-edge and the tip of your trowel to slice *right through* the mortar (not one-third of the way as with building blocks). The slits may appear to close but in fact do not.

(*c*) Knock away the frame boards after a further two or three days.

(*d*) These should come away cleanly leaving the slabs . . .

(*e*) . . . ready to be lifted by sliding the tip of a spade underneath their edges.

(*f*) They will snap apart cleanly at the slit marks and can then be stood on end to 'cure' for three further weeks. Do not use freshly made slabs before this or they will crack.

# INLAID PEBBLE DECORATION

Accurately shaped slabs must be cast in individual moulds, made from sound timber, and fastened together temporarily. An unusual finish can be given to them by hammer-inlaying of pebbles, known in most parts of Europe under the name of 'Waschbeton'.

(*a*) Fill the mould with mortar, as before, and beat the wet mortar down flat. Then, at once, take clean pebbles and scatter them over the surface.

(*b*) Use the wood again to beat the pebbles down into the surface. They will disappear under cement liquid but do not worry about this. Leave the slab for twenty-four hours.

(*c*) Then flood the surface with clean water . . .

(*d*) . . . and use a short-bristled stiff brush to scrub the pebbles clean. Repeat this flooding and scrubbing until the pebbles stand clear of the surface without becoming loose. After four more days remove the wooden frame by striking one corner of it apart. The result will be a clean-edged and decorative-surfaced slab. The mould can be cleaned and re-used many times. To speed up production you can buy rapid-hardening cement that can be taken from the mould within minutes, or liquids that are added to the mortar for the same purpose.

a

b

c

d

# SANDBED PEBBLE-DASH CASTING

A more easily controlled method of producing pebble-dash inlays is to use *inverted sandbed casting*. This simple technique enables you to produce quite complicated patterns as we show here with these pleasing circular slabs.

(*a*) For circular moulds buy a hoop of iron 2in (5cm) wide and bent into a circle. The ends should *not* be welded together but slotted so that they can be separated easily. Any blacksmith or metal worker will be able to produce such a ring quite cheaply.

(*b*) Within this ring spread a $\frac{1}{4}$in (6mm) layer of fine soft sand.

(*c*) Smooth this out evenly with a piece of timber.

a

b

◀

c

▶

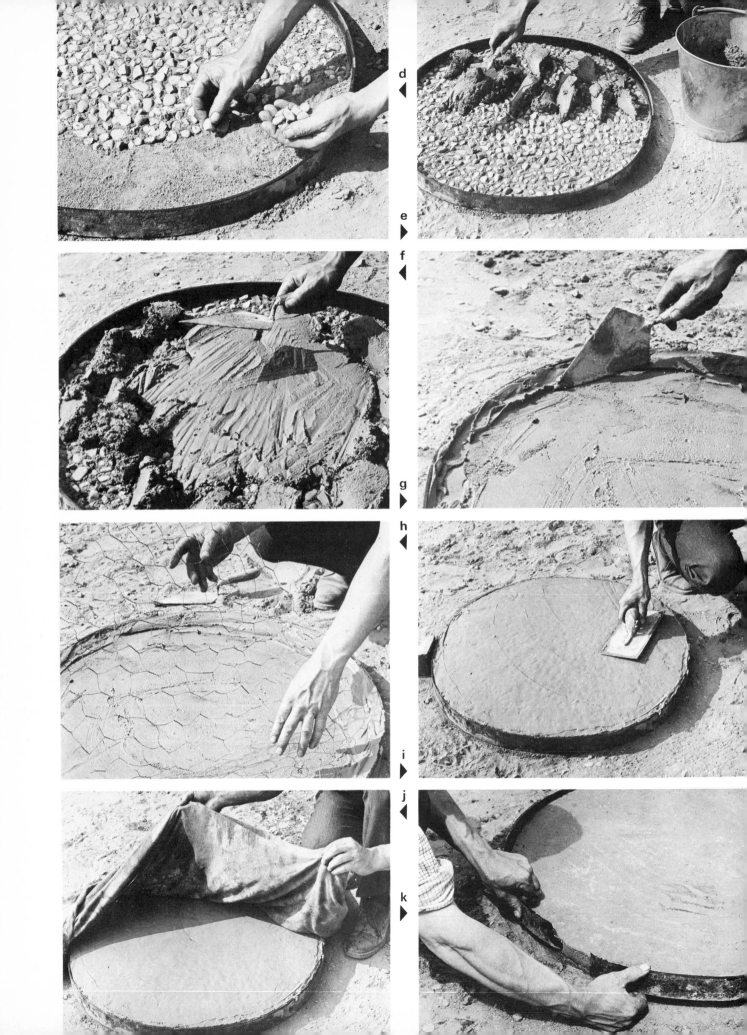

d

e

f

g

h

i

j

k

(d) Press decorative pebbles lightly halfway into the sand bed. You can place these at random, or in patterns.

(e) Mix mortar in the usual way and carefully place this over the pebbles, taking care not to disturb them.

(f) Beat the moist mortar down . . .

(g) . . . and smooth it firmly, especially at the mould edges.

(h) Such large, thin slabs need reinforcement. Cut a piece of ordinary wire netting to size and place it within the mould. Shovel further mortar on top of it.

(i) Smooth this off flush with the top of the mould.

(j) Protect the wet mortar from hot sun and frost with damp sacking.

(k) After a week, split the mould at the joint and spring the hoop of iron apart.

(l) Lift the slab gently from its sand bed and the pebbles will be found embedded in its surface.

(m) Brush away any surplus sand.

(n) Flood the surface with water . . .

(o) . . . and scrub the pebbles to bring up their texture.

# MOULDED SCREEN-BLOCK CASTING

There are many different patterns of decorative blocks for building garden walls. Not all can be easily made at home—many are complicated in design and need metal moulds. However, others *can* be cast in simple, easy-to-make wooden moulds.

The same general method will serve for several different shapes.

The concrete used is as usual a mortar of three parts of sand to one part of cement. Mix this fairly dry, preferably using water in which a 'plasticiser' has been added. Not only does this liquid make the mortar smooth and easier to work with, but it also helps to produce smooth and attractive surfaces on the blocks.

You can buy coloured cements or dyes to make blocks of different colours—but take care not to produce too gaudy effects. Blues, reds and greens often look unpleasant. A soft golden sandstone shade is pleasing. Pure white blocks are made with special white cement and pale-coloured sand.

Where speedy production is essential use rapid-setting cement or add chemicals that speed up setting (you can buy these from any builders' merchants). With high-speed mortars you can take blocks from the moulds only an hour or so after casting. However, they still remain fragile: all concrete takes several weeks to reach its full strength and should be treated gently during this time. Some shapes may require reinforcement with embedded lengths of thick galvanised wire, such as that sold for fencing.

### CONSTRUCTING THE MOULD

(*a*) To make the mould, you need a baseboard of heavy plywood at least ½in (1.5cm) thick, and rather larger than the block to be made. Then saw a planed timber plank to the

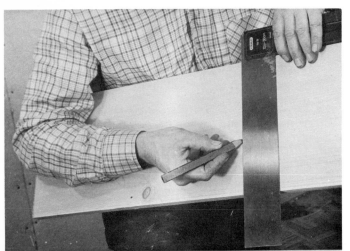

a

b

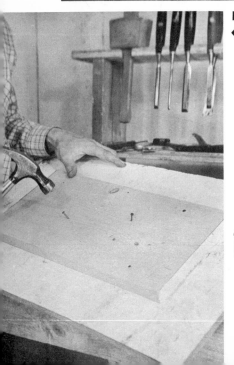

c

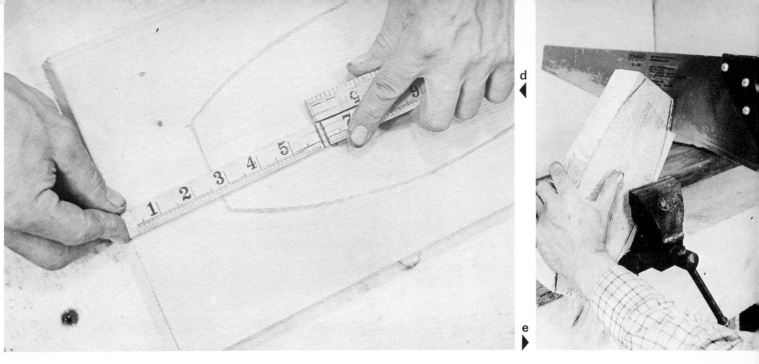

exact *length* and *height* of the finished block. Use a setsquare to make sure that the ends are an exact right angle.

(*b*) Nail this plank firmly to the centre of the baseboard.

(*c*) Mark on the plank the shape of the centre opening for the block.

(*d*) Accuracy of size and placing is essential. Errors in the mould will be repeated in all your blocks. Measure the markings to make sure they are centrally placed.

(*e*) Next take two or three blocks of thicker wood and saw them to the approximate size of the internal hole.

(*f*) Nail these boards together until you have reached the desired *thickness* of block.

(*g*) Finish this interior block with a plane to produce a smooth rounded surface. It must be tapered upwards, so that its top face is smaller than its lower face. This makes it much easier to extract the blocks from the moulds.

(*h*) Sandpaper the block perfectly smooth on all sides.

(*i*) Then screw it precisely in place on the bottom board. Use heavy screws driven in from the back, because this block must be held very firmly.

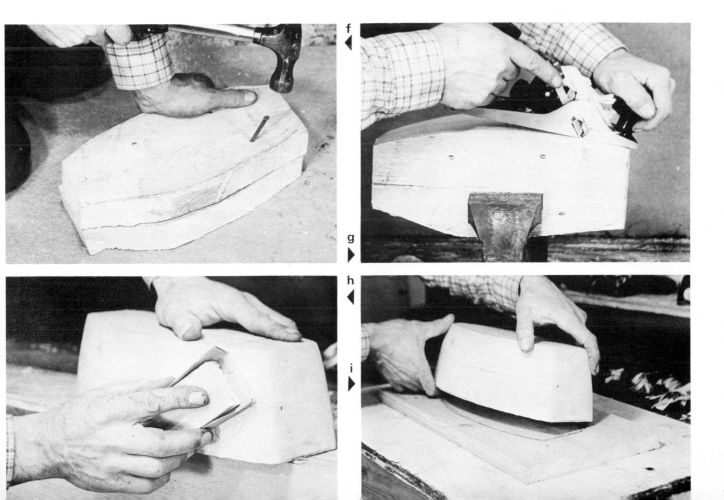

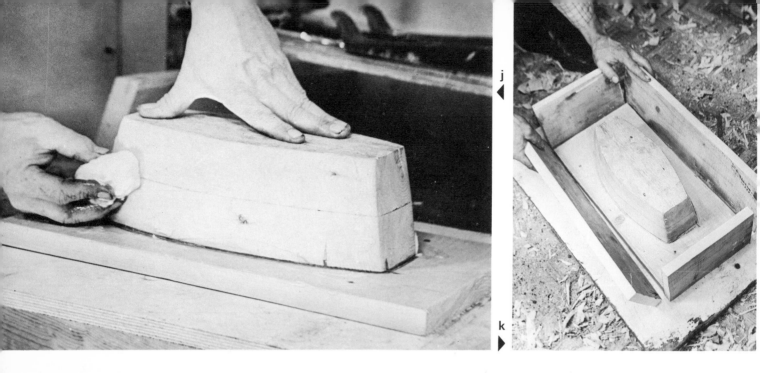

(*j*) Finally, grease the block and baseboard. Ordinary cooking fat will serve for this.

(*k*) The sides of the mould are made from planed planks of a height great enough to give a block of the desired thickness. Place the four pieces around the outside of the bottom plank.

(*l*) Three corners of this 'box' are hinged together with T-hinges placed on the outside. Note that the hinge pivot pins are *outside* the box.

(*m*) The fourth corner is held together with hooks and eyes, so holding the sides firmly about the base-block.

(*n*) Before use, grease also the interior sides of the mould.

## BEATING IN THE MORTAR

(*o*) Half-fill the mould with mortar . . .

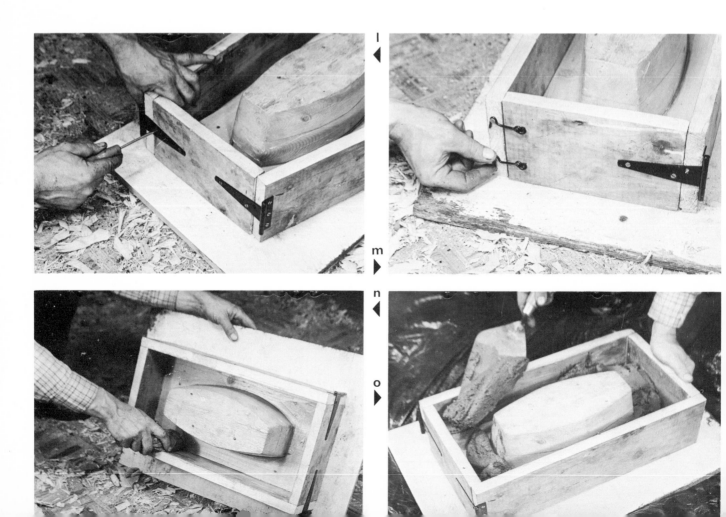

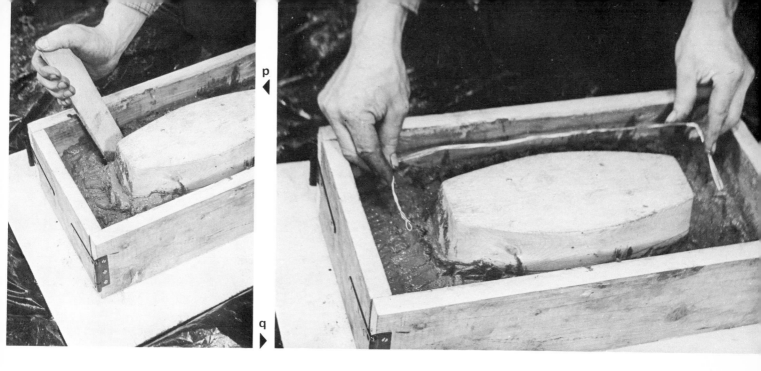

(*p*) . . . and beat it well down with a short length of wood. Continue beating until every trace of air has been expelled from the mortar.

(*q*) Reinforcements of twisted wire can now be pressed into the still-wet mortar.

(*r*) Finally fill the mould completely, beating the upper surface flat with the wood.

(*s*) Hammer lightly the sides of the mould to consolidate the mortar and give a smooth outer face. Place the block aside to set. With rapid-drying concrete this may be only an hour or even less. Ordinary cement mortar will take from one to three days (depending on the temperature).

### RELEASING THE BLOCK

(*t*) After this unhook the corner . . .

(*u*) . . . and remove the four outer planks. A sharp tap with a hammer may help. The concrete will remain firm and neat on the baseboard.

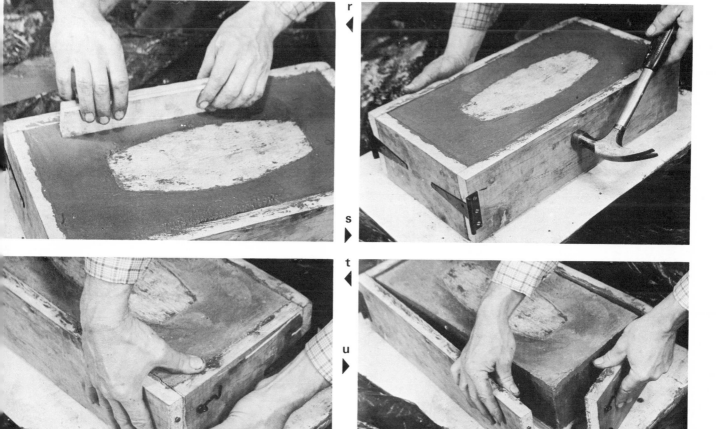

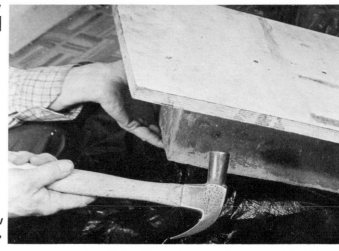

(*v*) The core will probably still be gripped firmly by the concrete.

(*w*) Free this by striking the mould and baseboard sharply, in several different places, whilst holding the block up with your other hand. *Never strike the concrete itself.* At this stage it will be quite fragile.

(*x*) The core should come cleanly away leaving the completed block with a smooth, even surface.

(*y*) Scrape the mould clean, re-grease and re-assemble.

(*z*) Minor irregularities on the block can be removed without difficulty at this stage with a shaping tool or file. By using an angular or rectangular core, blocks of different shapes can be made.

After maturing for about three weeks these blocks can be used. Protect them from frost during this time.

# CASTING AND CUTTING CAPPINGS AND KERBS

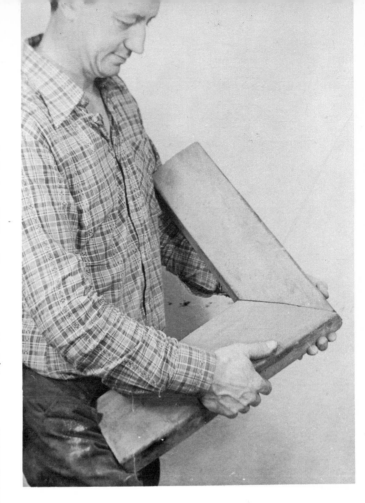

The tops of all garden walls must be protected with some form of capping. Concrete cappings are easily made and the most popular type has a peaked top to carry rainwater away. At the sides of paths narrow blocks are needed as kerbs.

These are best made in a metal mould. Even if you have no proper metalworking tools you can easily make a mould in aluminium, which is soft and easy to handle.

For speed, you can cast two blocks at once, in a mould 3ft (1m) long. The concrete used must not be too wet.

## THE ALUMINIUM MOULD

(*a*) Buy a piece of aluminium 1ft wide and 3ft long (about 30 × 100cm). Mark it with four lines, spaced 1½in and 3in (3.5 and 7cm) from each edge. Then lay a straight strip of

wood with one edge right down the exact *centre* of the aluminium. Wearing strong gloves, gently bend the metal along its centre line. Press the wood firmly down with the left hand whilst working gently along. Make the bend the exact angle required for the peaked top of your capping.

(*b*) Move the guide wood sideways to the inner pencil lines and fold the metal *up* to make a channel the width of the required capping. A wooden mallet makes a neat fold.

(*c*) Fold the metal outwards at the remaining marks, so producing the shape shown. Adjust for width and height.

a

b
◀

c
▶

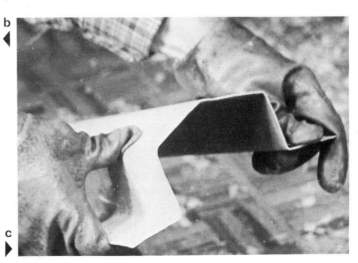

123

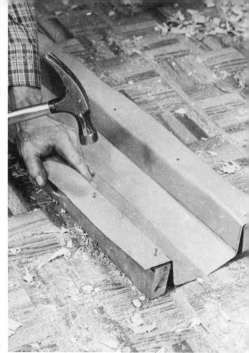

(d) Support both sides of the mould by placing the aluminium channel over two lengths of 2in (5cm) timber.

(e) Drive short nails through the metal to hold it in place.

(f) Finally, fold over any overlapping metal for safety.

(g) Nail a short length of wood across each end.

## DOUBLE CASTING

(h) Casting is done with the mould laid on any flat surface, but use plastic sheet to protect it against mortar drips. Lay an inch or two of mortar within the mould . . .

(i) . . . and beat it down firmly. Fill the mould up completely, levelling it with a wood strip tapped over the surface.

(j) After the concrete has started to set slice through the exact centre of the mould with the edge of your trowel. This slit will remain open, so the long capping will split in two.

(k) Once the concrete has fully set, tap the sides of the mould with a hammer . . .

i

j

k

l

(*l*) . . . and the cappings will fall clear. Clean the mould at once for further use.

## SHAPING

(*m*) Rough edges or irregularities can be easily trimmed off with a shaping tool or file, provided this is done immediately after casting.

(*n*) At this stage you can in fact shape the cappings quite considerably. It is possible to *saw* them, using any old, large-toothed saw. Naturally, sawing concrete wears saw blades, but there is no easier way of getting accurate mitred corners for cappings.

(*o*) The result will be a clean cut, easily smoothed off finally with a shaping tool. Mitres like this will fit together perfectly at the corners of walls.

As with all concrete castings, cappings and kerbs must be stored for three weeks to reach full strength before being erected.

m

n

o

# STONE STEPS IN
# THE GARDEN

Fully shaped and sawn slabs for garden steps are expensive but you can make a good job using ordinary quarry stone. Sandstone or limestone are best because they break into conveniently flat blocks. The simplest of all 'designs' is to place thick large blocks as solid steps embedded in the soil (see photograph below). This is really only suitable for informal paths and low flights; elsewhere steps should be built in masonry.

## PRELIMINARIES

You need a supply of thick blocks for the risers and rather thinner slabs for the treads of the steps. The exact *weight* of stone per square yard varies considerably. The amount to order should be discussed with your supplier.

The exact size of each step depends upon the angle of the slope and the number in the flight. There is a simple rule for making a comfortable size of step. This is that *twice the*

**a** ◀

**b** ▶

*height of a step* added to its width should equal about 26in (65cm). Supposing that the total height of each step is, say, 6in (15cm) then the width of each tread should be 14in (35cm).

(*a*) First remove all grass from the slope, peeling away the turf and removing the soft black top soil beneath. Then roughly excavate the shape of the steps into the soil. Each step should be dug approximately 8in (20cm) deeper into the bank than the finished step is to be. This allows for the thickness of the risers.

## A FOUNDATION

(*b*) At the bottom of the flight excavate at least 6in (15cm) deep to provide a solid foundation.

(*c*) Ram into this trench a 4in (10cm) layer of rubble, broken bricks and so on.

(*d*) Over this spread a layer of mortar (made with one part of cement to every three parts of coarse concreting sand). This layer should be below the finished level by the thickness of the stone paving, plus $\frac{1}{2}$in (1cm) or so for bedding mortar. Level it with a short length of board.

## TREADS AND RISERS

(*e*) Allow the base concrete to dry for about three days. Then spread a softer mortar 1in (2.5cm) deep over the surface. This time it is best to use soft building sand rather than the hard concreting variety. Draw mortar right up the *ends* of the excavation: all steps need support at the sides to prevent the adjacent soil slipping down onto the treads. Press stones into the still-moist end mortar so that their tops are at the correct angle.

**c**

**d**

**e**

27

f

g

(*f*) Then make the bottom tread with pieces of stone fitte together like crazy paving. Press them down into the moi cement and tap them level with the butt of a hammer.

(*g*) Use a small trowel to smooth the cement that rises i the joints. Preferably allow this base step to harden befor starting on the first riser.

(*h*) Spread a layer of mortar (again made with soft san about 1in (2.5cm) deep over the rear of the tread. Note th this mortar should preferably be *on top* of the stones of th tread. The next riser will then become cemented solidl with it.

(*i*) Choose your riser blocks carefully, using the thicke pieces and sorting them out so that they are approximatel even in thickness. Press them well down into the we mortar. The riser height will be the step height *less* the thick ness of the tread and its mortar bedding.

(*j*) Small pieces and off-cuts are then used behind th riser blocks as fillers, each being well cemented to the res

h

i

j

Finally fill any gap at the rear with well-rammed soil.

(*k*) When the riser has been completed, spread a $1-1\frac{1}{2}$in (2.5–4cm) layer of mortar over the entire next tread . . .

(*l*) . . . place the end supports as before . . .

(*m*) . . . and then lay the next tread edge. The front edge of each tread overhangs the riser by approximately $\frac{3}{4}$in (2cm). These stones should be particularly well cemented together as they will have to take most of the wear.

(*n*) Continue the steps upwards until the flight is complete, building each succeeding riser on top of the tread below. Then mortar all the joints and fill them up nearly flush with the face of the stone. A good brushing will remove dry surplus mortar but try to avoid getting raw cement on natural stone. It sometimes causes stains.

(*o*) Do not use the steps for at least one week, preferably not for three, to allow the mortar to harden thoroughly.

# STEPS IN CONCRETE

For steps that have to carry heavy traffic nothing is stronger or more hardwearing than solid cast concrete. These are not difficult to make, though the mixing of concrete takes time and effort. The diagrams below give the idea in principle. Planks are fixed across the front of each 'step' and these are filled up behind with a strong concrete, well rammed down. After a week the boards are removed. Note that a gap is left under each support board so that eventually all the steps form one solid block. Reinforcement is not usually necessary.

For garden steps you may prefer a coloured cement in a soft sandstone shade rather than the coldness of plain grey concrete.

If the steps are to have walls up each side these should be built first and the concrete cast solidly between them.

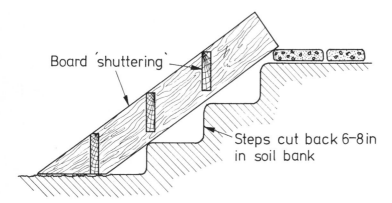

Board 'shuttering'

Steps cut back 6–8 in in soil bank

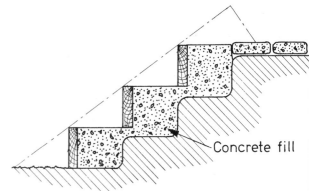

Concrete fill

# WOOD IN THE GARDEN

Unsawn or roughly trimmed timber looks well in the garden. But the use of such timber does *not* mean that the work should be clumsy or haphazard. Certainly the perfect joints used in furniture making are out of place but for maximum strength and durability the various parts must fit together reasonably accurately. Fungus rot usually starts at the sawn end-grain of damp wood, so closely fitting joints help to keep water out, and all saw-cuts need a coat of heavy protective paint. Of course, much garden woodwork is done without these refinements, which accounts perhaps for the poor state of many existing structures.

The commonest material is straight softwood, from firs, larches and so on. Other wood, such as gnarled branches of old oak trees, can be used with great effect; but for the novice, straight-grained lengths of wood are far easier to handle.

The bark of trees that have been felled in winter will usually remain firmly in place for many years but trees felled in spring or summer have less firmly attached bark and it is best to peel it off, otherwise it will rapidly flake and look unsightly. Peeled or sawn wood must be soaked in fungicide and later given one or two coats of heavy, outdoor-grade, clear varnish or paint. Bark does itself give some protection to the wood and if the wood is sound it is not then always necessary to treat it, but parts of posts that are underground will not survive more than a year or two unless they have been treated exceptionally heavily with preservative. Any buried wood must have two coats of heavy bituminous paint and this should extend at least 6in (15cm) *above* ground level.

When buying rustic poles always order at least a 20 per cent surplus so that you have an adequate choice of thin and thick material. Poles vary from about 1½in (4cm) up to 5in (12cm) in diameter and in lengths up to 20ft (7m) or even more. The wood tapers, and those parts of the structure which will be under the greatest strain must naturally be made from the thicker ends. Posts for fencing, for example, should never be less than 4in (10cm) in diameter at their *thinnest* point. This means for a 6ft (2m) length the butt will be about 6in (15cm) thick.

For really permanent work it is best to give posts a steel or concrete underground support to which the wooden uprights are then bolted. By keeping the timber clear of the ground in this way rot can largely be prevented. Another method for reducing future difficulties is to tie or bolt structures onto posts, which are replaced when bases rot.

The *upper* end of posts is also subject to rot caused by dampness soaking in, followed by fungus attack. Here protection can be given simply by putting a smooth slope on the top of the post to allow rain to run off. A better alternative is to fit wooden caps over the tops of the posts (see page 135).

Nails are best for fastening garden timber work together. It is extremely difficult to use woodscrews effectively, and they would often have to be uncomfortably large. Wherever there is likely to be strain, nails should be driven clean through the wood pieces and their tips bent over. This 'clenching' of nails adds to the strength of the structure. Blunt the nail ends with hammer blows to reduce the risk of splitting the wood: blunt points burst *through* the fibres rather than force them apart. Really large nails in important places should have guide-holes drilled beforehand. Steel nails, either round or oval, are normally used. Galvanised nails are even better, though more expensive, but must not be used with oak, which they tend to stain.

a

b

# HOW TO WORK WITH RUSTIC TIMBER

### PREPARING AND PAINTING

(*a*) A spokeshave removes bark easily, but an ordinary stiff-bladed knife will also do the job.

(*b*) A Surform shaping tool is almost ideal for finishing off the surface of the wood. It rides easily over minor irregularities and gives a relatively smooth even surface.

(*c*) Paint peeled rustic work with wood-preservative fungicide and two coats of outdoor-grade varnish. Use a broad brush.

(*d*) To saw thick wood without splitting the ends, first saw one-third of the diameter. Then turn the pole over and complete the cut from the top.

(*e*) All bases of posts should be painted. Use two heavy coats of bitumen or other good wood preservative. Bring the paint 6in (15cm) above soil level.

### MAKING A SCARF JOINT

(*f*) To join lengths of rustic pole end to end, saw both ends at a very acute angle. Make the cut three times as long as the diameter of the poles.

(*g*) Coat the cut ends with heavy water-proofing fungicidal paint.

(*h*) To prevent thick nails splitting the wood, blunt them by hammering their points.

(*i*) Drive several nails through the two pieces till the tips emerge at the other side. Then hammer ('clench') these over to give extra strength.

(*j*) Smooth the joint neatly. This joint looks best if the joined poles are of the same diameter.

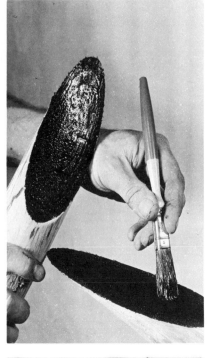

f

g

### MAKING A T-JOINT

(*k*) A T-joint is used to fasten one piece to another at right angles, for example a top rail to a post. First saw a V-notch in the post top. The exact size and angle of the V will depend on the size of the rail to be applied.

(*l*) For best appearance use a shaping tool or knife to take off smoothly the extreme edges of the V-notch.

(*m*) Coat the hollow in the post top with bitumen paint . . .

(*n*) . . . and drive substantial nails through at an angle. Two or three long thin nails at an angle make a stronger joint than one heavy nail driven in straight.

(*o*) The final result is a well-fitting T-joint in which water has little chance to collect and cause rot.

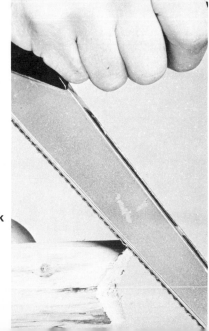

k

l

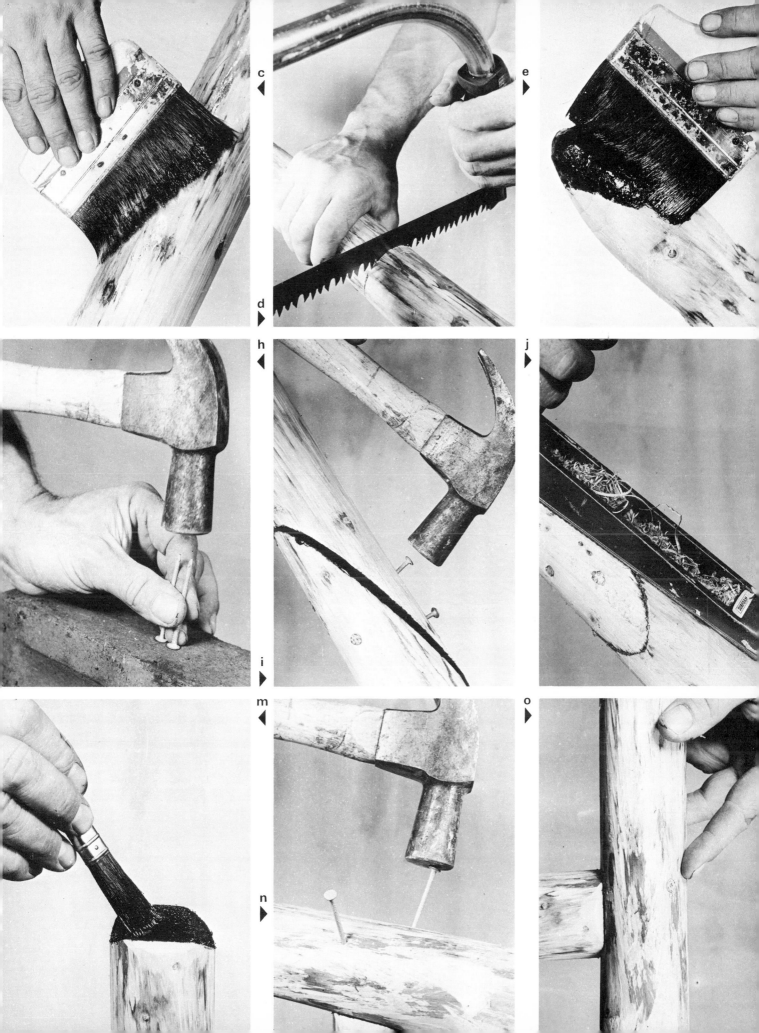

c ◄
d ►
e ►
h ◄
j ►
i ►
m ◄
o ►
n ►

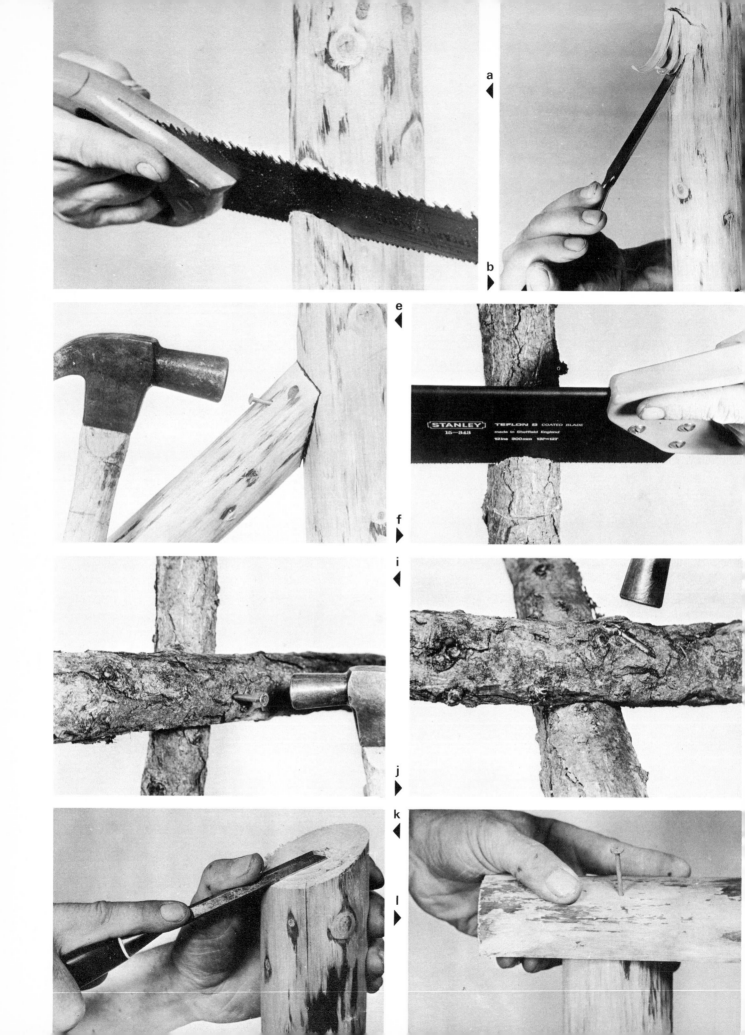

a

b

e

f

i

j

k

l

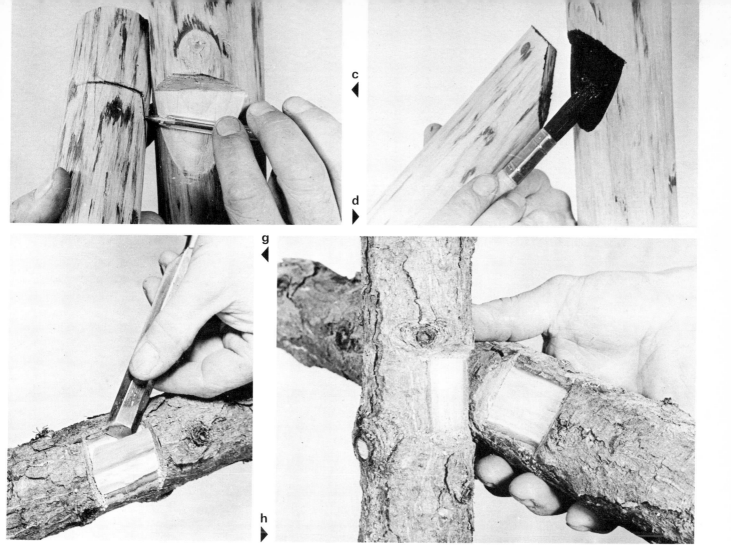

## MAKING AN ANGLED JOINT

(*a*) Where two parts meet at an angle you will need first to cut a notch into the post. Start by sawing inwards and downwards to about one-quarter of the thickness of the post and at the exact place where the other part is to fit.

(*b*) Then chisel out a notch up to this saw-cut at a fairly shallow angle.

(*c*) Place the second part in place holding it firmly, and use a pencil laid across the notch to mark it to the correct shape. Saw the part off at these angles.

(*d*) Check to see that it beds accurately and coat the cut surfaces with fungicide paint.

(*e*) Secure the joint with thin, blunted nails.

---

## POST-TOP PROTECTION

(*k*) At the very least, exposed post-tops must be sloping, and pared smooth with a chisel. Then coat with bituminous and other preservative paint.

(*l*) Better still, add short pieces of split rustic pole nailed across, using bitumen inside the joint. The rounded upper surface gives an excellent run-off for the rain.

135

## A CROSSOVER JOINT

Where two parts cross each other they may of course be simply nailed together. But it is best to prepare a 'foundation' for the rail, by removing the bark and some of the wood.

(*f*) Where the rail is to cross make marks about two-thirds of its diameter apart and saw inwards from these, sloping the saw at a considerable angle.

(*g*) Chisel away the bark and wood to give a flat 'bed'.

(*h*) Similarly prepare the other part, so that the faces bed neatly together.

(*i*) Coat the depressions with protective paint and drive a nail clean through the crossing points.

(*j*) Hammer over its tip till it re-enters the wood.

# A RUSTIC BENCH

This strong and serviceable garden bench is made with hammer and saw, using only the T-joint (pages 132–3). The wood is straight, moderately thick, rustic pole and all nails are 5 or 6in (12.5 or 15cm) round-headed steel. You will also need a little wood preservative for the joints.

(a) First cut four legs 12in (30cm) long, and saw shallow V-notches at the top of each. Each pair, front and rear, are T-jointed to a cross rail 1ft (30cm) shorter than the overall length of the bench. Fasten these rails roughly 3in (8cm) above the ground.

(b) For the seat take two lengths of rustic pole, and T-joint them to a short piece in the middle. The exact length of this spacer piece will depend on the thickness of the rustic but the overall width of the seat should be 12–13in (30–33cm).

(c) Across the ends of the seat nail end-pieces about 15in (38cm) long.

(d) Nail the seat into the V-notches at the tops of the legs.

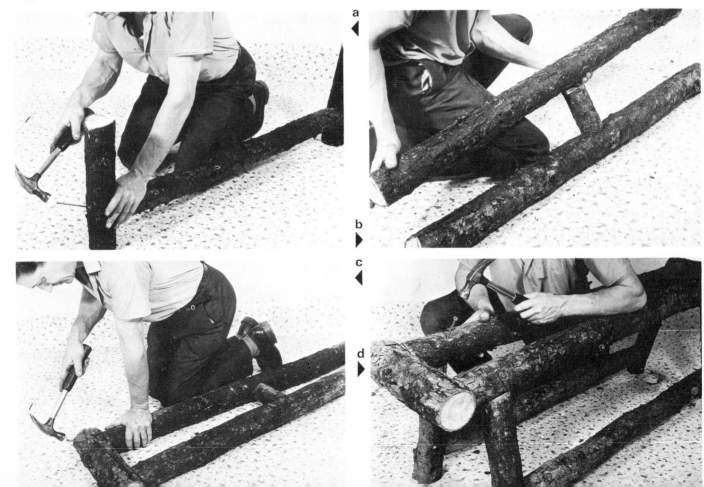

a

b

c

d

Note that the leg frames here are splayed outwards a little at the base for better appearance. Their bottom ends must naturally be cut at a slight angle to bed solidly to the ground.

(*e*) Between the bottom rails fit suitably cut lengths of rustic pole well nailed from front and back.

(*f*) The seat planks are of $3 \times 1\frac{1}{2}$in (7.5 × 4cm) sawn timber—more comfortable than rustic pole. Space them equally.

(*g*) Nail them in place and smooth off the ends. There is no need to make a perfect finish but any sharp snags should be removed. All exposed wood should be thoroughly treated with wood preservative, either colourless or staining.

(*h*) Shorter or longer seats can be made, but the height should not vary much.

# A RUSTIC TABLE

The rustic table shown on page 136 (*top left*) is designed to give the maximum strength and rigidity, but only the T-joint (pages 132–3) and crossover joint (pages 134–5) are used in its construction.

(*a*) Cut four equal leg pieces roughly 3ft (1m) long. Saw their upper ends into shallow V-notches and their lower ends with a 45° slope. Crossover joint them at the middle.

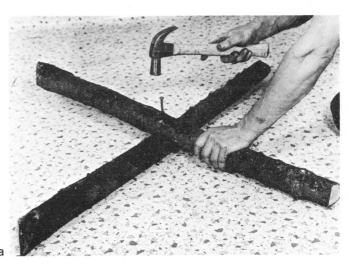

(b) Stand the leg crosses upside-down on a flat surface. Lay a length of pole between them and nail it strongly into their *lower* angle. Drive at least two nails into each leg from the rail, and two more into the rail from each leg.

(c) Turn the leg crosses right way up and fit lengthways rails across the tops of each pair, using T-joints.

(d) Then join these rails with a cross piece, strongly nailed.

(e) The rigidity of the frame comes largely from the fitting of diagonal braces as shown here. These stretch from the centre of the cross piece at the top to the junction of the leg crosses at each end. Make them a tight fit and nail the ends securely.

(f) Space out the table top planks of $8 \times 1$ in ($20 \times 2.5$ cm) wood with 1 in (2.5 cm) gaps between to allow the rain to pass freely through them. Nail them down using dovetail nailing in which alternate nails are leaned away from each other.

(g) Finally straighten and smooth off the edges of the top strips and any projections on the rustic poles.

# A RUSTIC CHAIR

This simple but strong rustic chair uses only the T-joint (pages 132–3) and crossover (pages 134–5).

## THE FRAME

(a) Cut four leg-pieces, 12in (30cm) long, and joint them by a cross piece in rather thinner pole about 15in (38cm).

(b) Across the top of each pair of legs fasten a cross piece as shown here, both ends V-notched for T-jointing.

(c) Between the lower cross pieces nail a length of rustic pole approximately 16in (40cm) long.

(d) Then nail front and rear rails of the seat to the prepared ends of the upper cross pieces.

(e) At the rear of the seat nail two verticals to support the back. Notice that these verticals are T-jointed to the *lower* cross piece between the legs, but crossover jointed behind the *upper* cross piece. This will make the uprights lean backwards slightly.

(f) The nails used to fasten the uprights must be long enough to pass through both pieces of wood. Hammer them over at the tips. This clenching is essential.

(g) Across the top of the uprights fit a rustic rail.

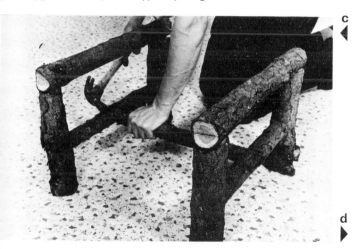

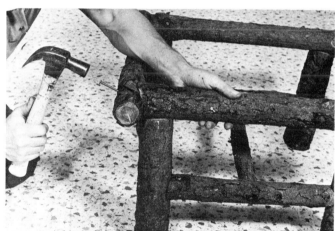

## BUILT-IN STRENGTH

(*h*) To brace the entire structure, T-joint two diagonals between the upper front cross piece and the lower rear cross piece. It is important to fit these no matter how rigid the structure may already appear to be. After a month or two of use an unbraced frame becomes too flexible.

(*i*) Here is the chair frame complete.

## ADDED COMFORT

(*j*) Make the seat and back with strips of planed 2 × 1in (5 × 2.5cm) wood, equally spaced across the frame and nailed to it securely by dovetail nailing.

(*k*) Round and smooth off the ends and front edge of the seat strips and sand the woodwork well.

(*l*) The completed chair is quite rigid and strong.

# A RUSTIC PLANT TROUGH

(*a*) Saw a number of equal lengths of rustic pole about 18in (45cm) long. Make a grid from six lengths nailed as shown, four in a square and two more spaced equally across this.

(*b*) Build up the trough by adding strips to opposite sides alternately until you have reached the desired height.

(*c*) A raised trough is made by nailing four legs of suitable length inside the corners. They look better if they are allowed to splay outwards a little.

(*d*) Line with fine mesh plastic or metal netting.

(*e*) When planting, line first with moss, then peat, and fill up with good potting compost. Regular watering will be needed as the container will dry out fairly rapidly.

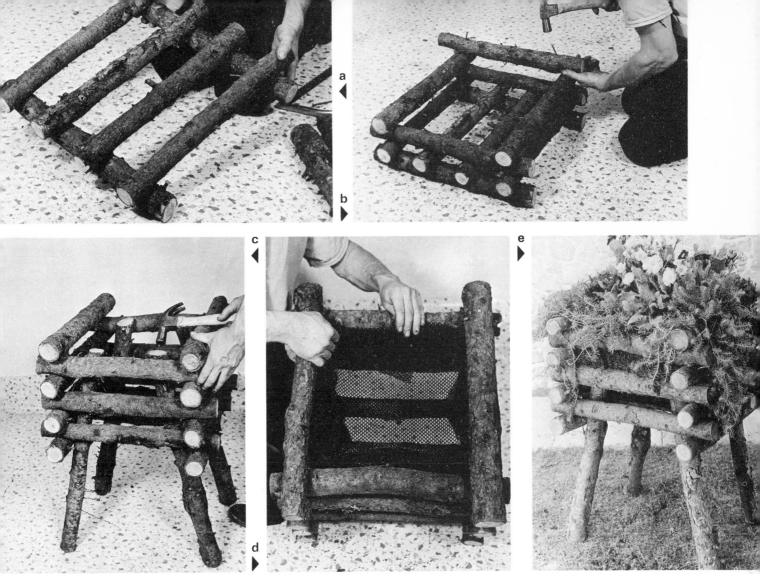

# A MODERN TIMBER SEAT

For modern gardens planed timber may be more suitable than rustic work. The design of seat shown here is simple to make and requires only a saw, hammer, file and sandpaper. The material is all $11 \times 1$in ($27 \times 2.5$cm) planed softwood. Cedarwood, which requires no painting yet will never rot, could be used instead. However, this type of seat often looks best if painted white. Several coats of paint will be needed and should be renewed at two- or three-year intervals. When painting cedar, always use an aluminium paint first, as a primer.

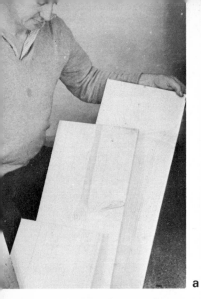

**a**

**b**

## FIRST THE ENDS

(*a*) Each seat end is made up with three pieces of timber 11in (27cm) wide and respectively 29in (73cm), 27in (68cm) and 13in (32cm) long.

(*b*) The rear upright is the 27in (68cm) piece. Saw a slanting section from the upper front part of this at a shallow angle 3in (8cm) wide at the top and 13in (32cm) long. This gives the slope for the back.

(*c*) The shortest piece is the front leg. Place it beside the rear leg but some 5in (13cm) apart from it.

(*d*) Lay the 29in (73cm) length across the two legs but at an angle to them. Its front top end should meet the front top of the front leg, and its rear lower end should meet the rear bottom of the rear leg.

(*e*) Shade the waste wood at the top of the front leg . . .

(*f*) . . . and at the front and rear end of the cross piece. Saw this waste away.

(*g*) Nail the three parts firmly together, angling the nails towards each other to give better grip.

(*h*) Make up the second end in the same way but note that the two ends are mirror images of each other and the cross piece must be on the *inside* in each case.

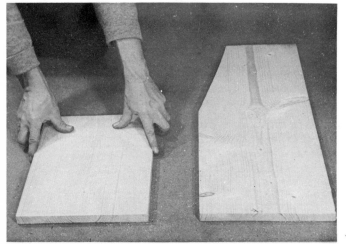

**c**

**d**

**f**

**e**

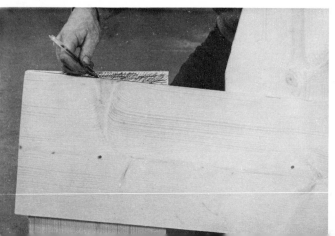

**g**

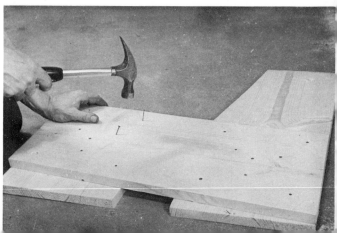

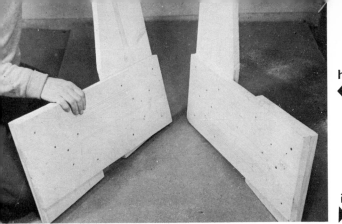

**h** ◄

**i** ►

**j** ◄

**k** ►

## JOIN WITH FRONT PLANK AND STRIPS

(*i*) Across the front, nail a further 11in (27cm) board the full length of the seat. The length can be from 24in for a single seat to about 4ft for a two to three seater (60–120cm).

(*j*) Measure the gap between the rear of the ends to make sure that the seat is properly aligned . . .

(*k*) . . . and then nail on seat pieces of 4 × 1in (10 × 2.5cm) timber spaced roughly 1in (2.5cm) apart.

(*l*) Continue up the back with other strips and then lay and nail an 8in (20cm) plank right across the top of the back.

(*m*) Round off the front of this, and the ends of the other planks, with a file or shaping tool.

(*n*) Sandpaper the whole seat and give it at least three coats of paint: primer, undercoat and gloss white.

**l**

**m** ◄

**n** ►

# MAKE YOUR OWN COMPOST CONTAINER

The best way to make compost is in a proper container which is easy to load and unload, and which allows free access to the air at the sides.

The one we show here is approximately 3ft (1m) high 3ft (1m) wide and a little over 2ft (60cm) deep. This is the smallest size for making good compost.

The construction is very simple and provided the wood is well treated with preservative it will give years of satisfactory service.

### FRONT, BACK AND ONE SIDE

(a) For the front of the container cut three 3ft (1m) lengths of wood, roughly 2 × 1in (5 × 2.5cm) in section. Space them out flat on the ground to cover an area 3ft (1m) wide. Then place over them a 3ft sq (1m sq) piece of heavy-gauge 1½in (4cm) mesh wire netting.

(b) Place two further 3ft (1m) pieces of timber across from side to side, so sandwiching the netting between these end strips. Nail the wood together at each crossing-place.

(c) Before completing the nailing, check that the work is a true square by measuring across the diagonals. *Both* should measure exactly the same.

(d) From top to bottom of the frame nail further strips of timber spaced roughly 3in (7.5cm) apart. This strong framework is essential because the full container will hold about a ton of compost. Make sure that the nailing is secure, using two nails, angled slightly towards each other, in every joint.

(e) Make a back frame in exactly the same way, and the rather narrower end frame similarly, but with only two uprights and with horizontals projecting 2in (5cm) at either side for nailing to the front and rear parts. Stand the frames, with the netting *inwards*, on rows of loose bricks (to keep the timber from contact with the soil).

a ◀

b ◀

c ▶

## THE OPEN END

(f) The other end is left open except for a heavy rail of
4 × 1in (10 × 2.5cm) timber securely nailed at the bottom ...

(g) ... and another across the top.

(h) As the compost heap is filled from this open end, more
planks of wood cut to fit behind the end uprights are simply
slotted into place. They are held there by the pressure of the
compost within. This side can be slowly raised till the
container is full. When the compost is to be turned or
removed it is easy to slide the boards out.

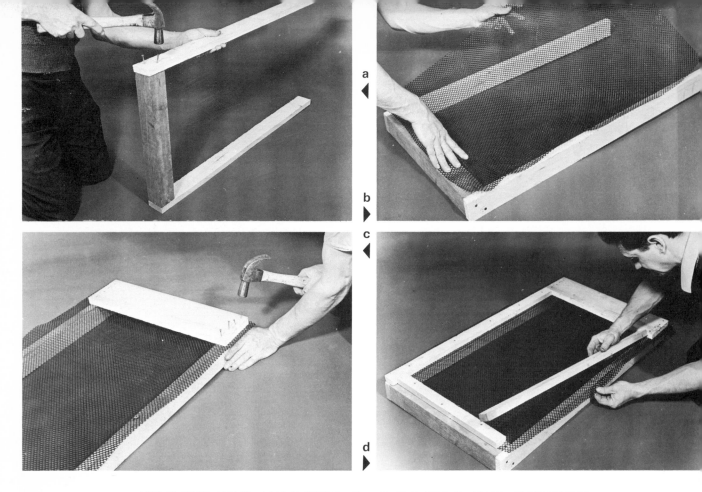

# HOW TO MAKE A COMPOST SIEVE

Compost for seed-growing and many other garden purposes must be sieved. This is easy with the device shown here.

(*a*) Take two lengths of wood each $2\frac{1}{2}$in × 1in × 3ft (7cm × 2.5cm × 1m) and nail them strongly to a piece 2 × 2 × 18in (5 × 5 × 45cm).

(*b*) Lay a sheet of suitable metal or plastic netting (Netlon 'Windbreak' plastic) over the partly completed frame.

(*c*) Across the other end of the frame, and over the netting, nail an 18in (45cm) length of 5 × 1in (12.5 × 2.5cm) wood.

(*d*) Nail strips of 1 × 1in (2.5 × 2.5cm) wood to the frame sides and ends, sandwiching the netting.

(*e*) Finally screw two short supporting legs to the frame sides to hold the sieve up at an angle.

(*f*) When the raw compost is thrown against the net the fine particles fall through and the coarse ones slide down to the ground to be shovelled up again.

(*g*) If the sieve is balanced on a barrow the fine material falls into the barrow, ready for transport to site.

# A USEFUL RAKING AND LEVELLING TOOL

Preparing seed beds for vegetable sowing or lawns can be a long and tricky operation. It may be easy enough to get the soil broken down into a fine condition but the last, perfect levelling is another matter. This simple wooden tool, fixed to your rake, will greatly help to get the soil perfectly flat.

Where plants are to be sown in straight, parallel drills these must be exactly the same distance apart for easy cultivation. The tool can be turned over to make a drilling hoe which draws out seed drills quickly and accurately.

(a) Take a length of timber approximately 3in × 1in × 3ft (7.5cm × 2.5cm × 1m). In its centre cut a notch large enough to accept the head end of your rake handle.

(b) Slide the rake, points downwards, into the slot, and fit a second length of similar timber about 15in (38cm) long on the other side of the rake. Drive strong woodscrews through the two pieces of wood to hold them firmly to the rake head.

(c) Next, nail several pegs of wood roughly 1 × 1 × 5in (2.5 × 2.5 × 12.5cm) along the length of the tool, the distance between each being the width required between drills.

(d) Use the back of the tool to make the vegetable bed level . . .

(e) . . . and then turn it over and draw it steadily through the soil to produce perfectly parallel drills, ready for seeding.

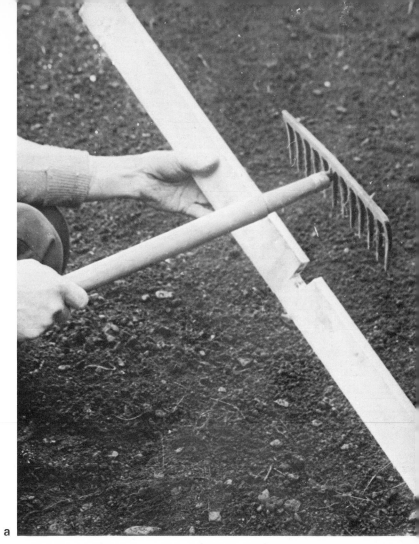

a

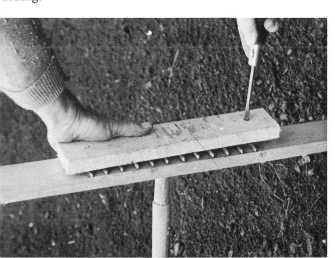

b ◀

c ▶

d ◀

e ▶

a

b

# A LARGE MITRE-TOOL
# FOR GARDEN WOODWORK

To make first-class right-angle joints in timber work you really need the help of a *mitre-box*. This is simply a box without ends or lid in which the wood can be laid. Pre-sawn slots in the box sides guide the saw at an angle of 45°.

Such boxes are commonly used in joinery but are rarely large enough to work with rustic pole or heavy wood. However, it is simple enough to make your own.

(*a*) The only materials you need are three straight timber lengths about $6 \times 2 \times 18$in ($15 \times 5 \times 45$cm). Place the three pieces together to form the sides and base.

(*b*) Nail the sides to the base very securely indeed.

(*c*) Now mark each side with two carefully drawn vertical lines, exactly as far apart as the overall width of the top of the box. If the measurement right across the top of the box

is 10in (25cm) then the distance between these two vertical lines should also be 10in (25cm).

(*d*) Lay a straight-edge diagonally across the top of the box between these lines and mark the tops of the sides at this angle. This will be a 45° marking. Saw down vertically along these lines. Take care to make this saw-cut perfectly. It is your guide for all future work so the angle must be accurate.

(*e*) When using a mitre-box, first lay a piece of waste timber in the bottom to prevent the box from being damaged.

(*f*) Hold the pole or timber to be sawn against the rear of the box *with the sawing position aligned with the diagonal cuts*. Saw down slowly, letting the saw cut move in the guide slots in the sides of the mitre box. In this way you will cut the end at exactly 45°.

c

d

e

f

# BUILDING A COLD FRAME

A garden frame is useful for producing early seedlings, propagating plants and caring for houseplants. It is not difficult to make one, although the work does require care.

The exact size can be varied somewhat to suit your needs. The one shown is roughly 4ft (120cm) square. It is simplest to use large sheets of glass but smaller pieces overlapped on each other and bedded in putty will be quite satisfactory.

## TAPERED SIDES

(*a*) Both sides are made together, using 7in (17cm) wide tongued and grooved timber. Tongues on one edge of the wood fit into slots in the edge of the adjoining plank. Cut six pieces each 33in (83cm) long and fit them in a rectangle.

(*b*) Across one end of the six planks, fasten a strip of wood about 2 × 1in (5 × 2.5cm) in section.

a
◄

b
►

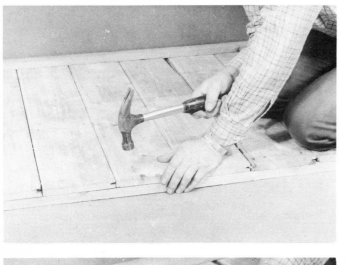

(*c*) At the opposite end, nail a similar strip of wood but *underneath the planks* instead of on top.

(*d*) Draw a line diagonally across the centre area of the rectangle of planking, joining points on opposite sides each 11in (27cm) from the reinforced edgings.

(*e*) Place strips of timber approximately 2in (5cm) square on either side of this line, *one strip above and one below*, with roughly $\frac{1}{8}$in (3mm) between them. Nail securely.

(*f*) The planking can now be sawn in two along the diagonal line, cutting *between* the inner strips to produce two tapering sides.

(*g*) Cut any overlapping ends flush with the ends of the planking.

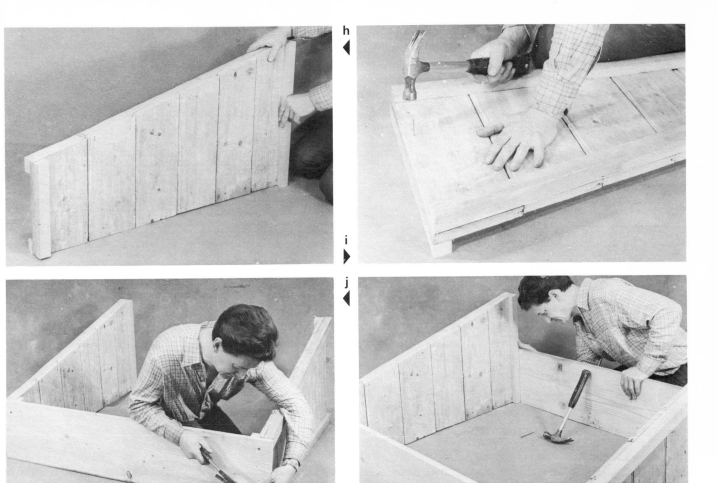

h ◀
i ▶
j ◀
k ▶

(h) Cut and fit 2in (5cm) square timber upright at the front and rear of these side pieces.

(i) Nail them solidly into position. These strips reinforce the frame corners.

## FRONT AND BACK

(j) The front of the frame is a single plank 11in (27cm) wide and 1in (2.5cm) thick nailed firmly to the sides.

(k) Make the rear of the frame from two similar planks nailed one above the other.

(l) File the top of the front plank to an angle to continue the slope of the sides, and the base is now complete.

## FRAME FOR THE GLASS

(m) For the glass top you need a top and bottom cross piece of planed wood, 2½in (7cm) square and 4ft (120cm) long, and three uprights to carry the glass, each 2½in × 2in × 4ft (7cm × 5cm × 120cm). These are grooved up the sides. You can buy ready grooved timber or alternatively groove your own with a slotting plane like the one shown here. This takes out a groove ¼in (6mm) wide and deep, along the narrower face of the wood.

l ◀
m ▶

n ◀

o ▶

p ◀

q ▶

r ▶

s ◀

t ▶

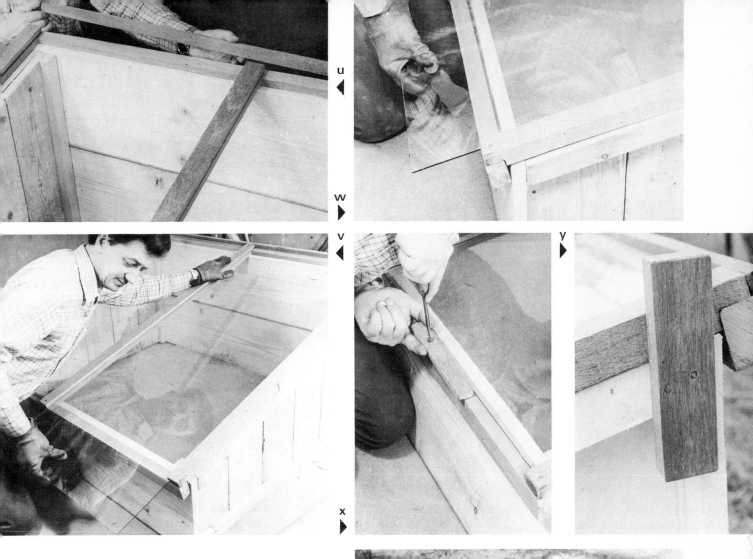

(n) To make the corner joints, overlap the uprights and cross pieces and mark alongside them with pencil lines.

(o) Take the uprights and saw down the pencil line to the edge of the groove.

(p) Saw from the *end* of the strip to meet the first saw cut . . .

(q) . . . and so take out a rebate as shown here.

(r) Fit the cross piece in the rebate and drill down through both from top to bottom.

(s) Use screws and nuts to fasten the corners.

(t) Make all joints of the frame in this way, checking that it fits exactly over the frame base.

(u) Fasten a $1\frac{1}{2} \times \frac{1}{2}$in ($4 \times 2$cm) strip of timber right across the upper end of the frame, to prevent the glass sliding past it.

(v) Slide suitably sized panes of glass up into the side slots.

(w) The glass rides over the top of the lower cross piece into the slots in the uprights.

(x) Hold the panes in place with strips of waste timber screwed to the bottom cross piece, next to the glass.

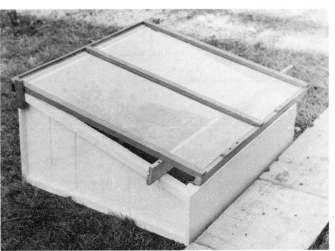

## WHEN IN USE . . .

(y) The upper frame simply rests on top of the base. To stop it sliding sideways, screw blocks to either side of the base.

(z) Fresh air is important to all plants under glass. A simple ventilation method is a board laid across the sides.

153

# CAST YOUR OWN PLANTING BOWL

Many of us would like to have a large concrete bowl in our gardens, perhaps for a fountain base, pool, or simply as a planting place for flowers. Yet to make round or oval moulds to cast such things is a highly skilled operation. Nonetheless by the remarkably simple method of working on a mould of sand you can produce attractive bowls in many shapes without any actual mould at all.

The *interior* shape of your bowl is moulded in soft, moist sand (rather as children make sand castles at the seaside). Then mortar is applied all round the heap, smoothed off and allowed to set. The completed bowl is lifted clear, cleaned off and the interior smoothed over with mortar. No special equipment is needed.

### MAKE A SAND MOULD

(*a*) Make a pile of sand and roughly shape it to the *interior* size of the bowl required. The sand should be moist enough to hold together smoothly when patted but not be wet or sloppy.

Use the trowel and the palm of the hand to smooth the heap into a neatly rounded mould.

(*b*) To mould the pile to the *exact* interior shape of the bowl, use a template. This is simply a piece of plywood, with the desired *interior* shape cut into its corner as shown here. Place the template end against a guide peg thrust in the centre of the heap and swing it round . . .

(*c*) . . . to produce an evenly shaped mould of sand with the guide peg in its centre.

### APPLY AND SHAPE THE MORTAR

(*d*) Take the shaped template and draw on it the *thickness* of the bowl that you require. This can be done by eye quite easily. The thickness should be greater at the base than at the rim. Cut it to this new shape.

(*e*) Mix your mortar moist but firm and lay it gently in trowelfuls right around the base and up the sides of the mould.

(*f*) Press downwards with the trowel to smooth the mortar without disturbing the sand.

(*g*) It is best to reinforce large bowls by cutting small patches of ordinary fine wire netting . . .

(*h*) . . . and pressing these into the still-wet surface of the mortar. Then apply more mortar above the netting, burying it.

(*i*) Use your shaper as a guide to see whether the final shape is correct.

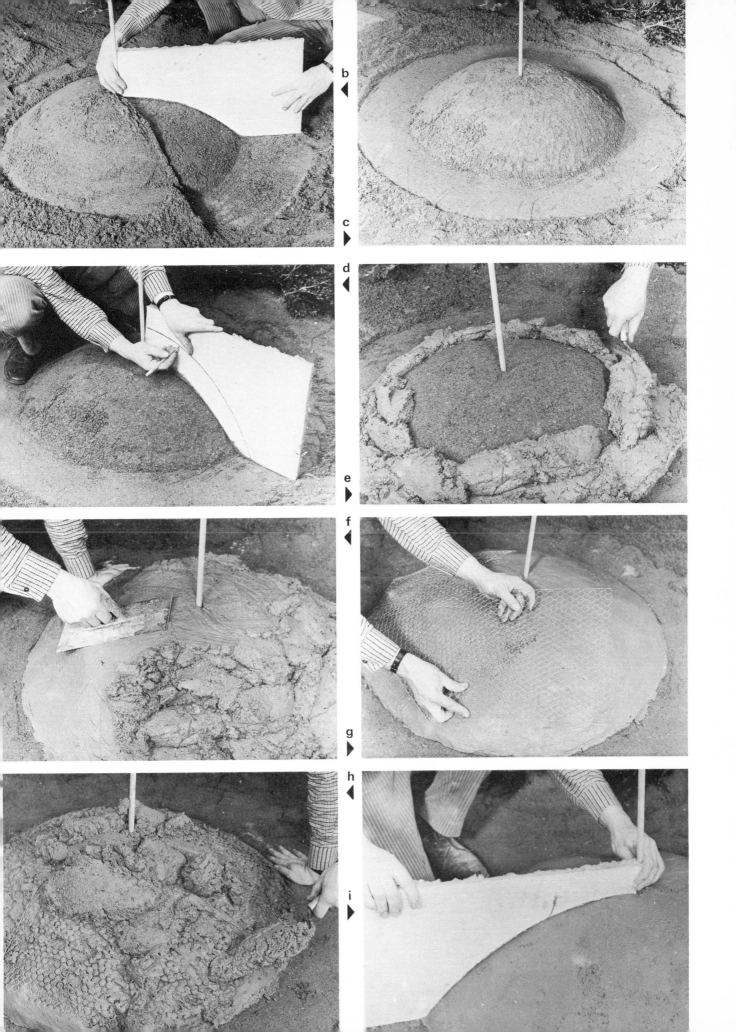

b

c

d

e

f

g

h

i

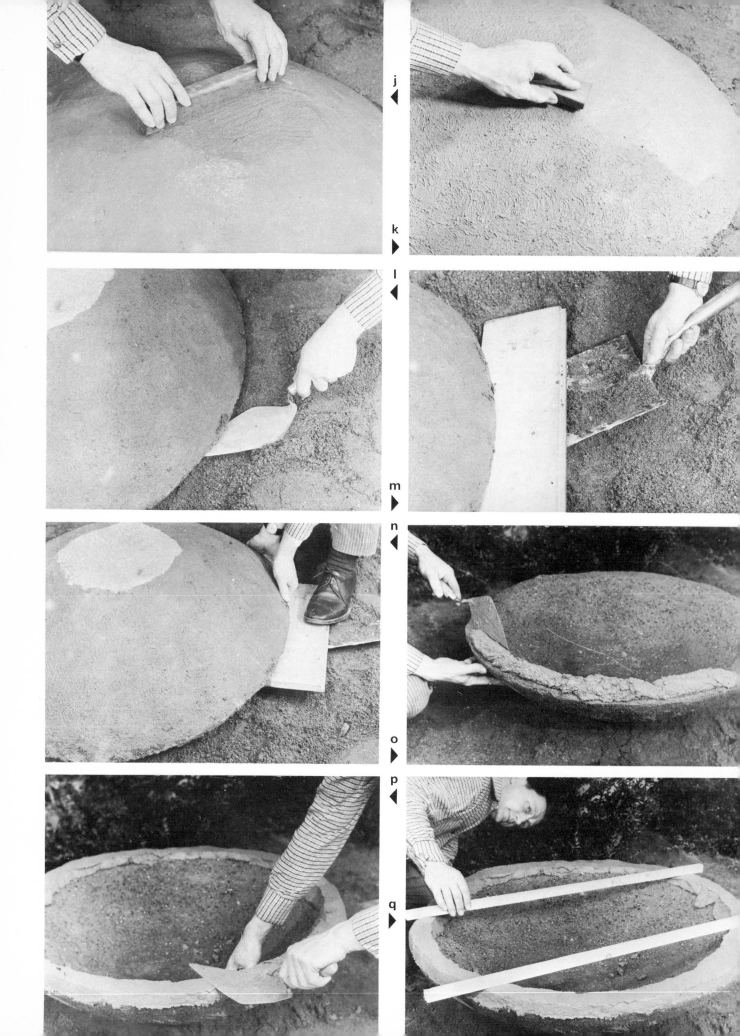

j

k

l

m

n

o

p

q

(*j*) Smooth over the entire exterior with your trowel, as neatly as possible, although absolute accuracy once again is not essential. If the bowl has to have a flat base now is the time to tap this flat gently, with the aid of a short piece of timber.

### FINISHING OUTSIDE AND IN

(*k*) Smooth finishes for these bowls are hard to achieve by an amateur, due to the curved surface. An equally attractive matt effect is produced by swirling a short, stiff brush over the moist surface of the mortar.

(*l*) Leave the bowl in position for at least ten days, longer in cold weather, protecting it from frost or extreme heat. Then remove the sand from beneath the edge with the tip of a trowel.

(*m*) Slide a board underneath its edge to protect it as you lever the bowl up from the mould with the tip of a spade.

(*n*) Once the mould is clear of the ground you can get your hands under it and gently turn the bowl right way up. Some sand will still stick to the interior of the bowl. Swill this

away with a good deal of clean water.

(*o*) Then apply a rim of new mortar round the rim . . .

(*p*) . . . and smooth off the top with the trowel.

(*q*) Sight across two strips of wood laid over the rim to see that the bowl top is not twisted.

(*r*) Smooth the interior with mortar . . .

(*s*) . . . smoothed off with the tip of the trowel . . .

(*t*) . . . and finished by swirling the stiff brush over the moist surface.

(*u*) Finally, round off the moist rim of the bowl with a soft hand brush. You will find it easy to make minor adjustments to the rim shape at this stage.

Leave the entire bowl to set for at least a month before attempting to plant it. If drainage holes ar required (for a planting bowl) these are best made in the early stages, whilst the casting is still wet, although freshly cast concrete can be readily drilled. If used for fountain bowls, use a waterproof cement, or add a waterproofing agent to the mixing water. Remember *not* to put fish into a freshly cast concrete bowl. The water draws poisons from the cement.

# THE GARDEN POOL

Water-gardening is a big subject, and we can only give a few hints here. Pools can be made in several different ways. The simplest is to purchase a ready-moulded fibreglass pool and drop it in a suitably shaped hole. Line the hole with soft sand first and pack this round the sides too. This prevents the pool shifting after fitting.

Another method is to line the sanded hole with sheets of plastic, held down round the edges with heavy stones. This gives a pool which with care will last for a number of years.

## CONCRETE IS BEST

Undoubtedly the most permanent method is to use concrete. For this excavate the soil 6in (15cm) deeper than the pool depth, and ram the base and sides firmly. Mix a water-proofed concrete and spread this in the hole and up its sides. This can be done in a similar way to casting a concrete bowl (page 154). Line the hole with sand, patted smooth, and then start from the centre and work outwards, applying trowelfuls of concrete and pressing them firmly against the sand. Take care not to get soil mixed with the concrete. Make this first layer roughly 1½–2in (4–5cm) thick and allow it to set with a *rough* surface. After a week, apply a further 3in (7.5cm) layer, pressing wire netting into it and finishing with a sheet of builder's 1000-gauge polythene. This should be big enough to line the pool in one sheet. Do not cut it to fit. Instead, fold it at the corners and up the sides. Finally add a further 1½in (4cm) of waterproof mortar (three parts of sand to one of cement) and smooth this carefully. Bring it right up over the polythene sheet edges to seal this completely from view.

Lay slabs or stones around the edges to soften the otherwise hard outlines. Pools made like this will last for many years.

Do not put in fish or plants for six months or poisons from the fresh concrete will injure them. Fill and refill the pool several times during this period. There are commercial paints to speed up the poison removal.

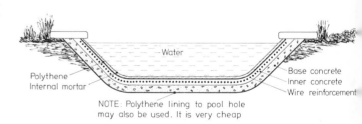

NOTE: Polythene lining to pool hole may also be used. It is very cheap

# WATERFALLS AND FOUNTAINS

Waterfalls and fountains can be arranged even in small pools by using pumps. These either force the water up an incline and allow it to fall down or spray it upwards directly from the pump.

In the first system the pumps are arranged *above* water level in a weatherproof box near the pool (see photograph below). A suction pipe draws water up and the outlet pipe leads it to the top of the waterfall. All these pipes are buried, both for concealment and for protection against frost.

In the second system the pumps are themselves waterproof and sunk below the water level, with their spray tops just above the surface (*bottom right*). Once switched on they force out fountains in various patterns without any further plumbing. Low voltage equipment is essential for this type.

In both cases, the electrical connections must be made by an expert electrician.

# PILLARS AND PERGOLAS

Most of the work shown in this book has been strictly fo[r] newcomers to garden building. This last item, howeve[r] shows the type of construction that can only be attempte[d] after a certain amount of practice. It calls for very accurat[e] building and special attention to the correct mixing o[f] mortar.

In principle, the pillars are made by arranging rectangula[r] concrete blocks around an inner core of steel rod (se[e] diagram below). The whole hollow centre of the pillar i[s] filled up solid with concrete, the rod being long enough t[o] project at least 18in (43cm) into deep concrete foundation[s] and up into the wooden cross pieces. All foundations mus[t] be twice as broad in each direction as the pillars, and left t[o] set for four weeks before building the pillars.

The pillars are built at least five weeks before the cros[s] pieces (*below right*) are put into place. These are then care[-] fully bedded in mortar and jointed tightly together. In thi[s] way each pillar supports its neighbour via the timber.

Pillars and pergolas may be too large for most garden[s] but they will not be beyond your ability to build once yo[u] have become experienced in the techniques outlined in th[is] book.

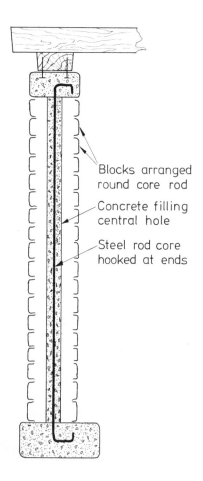

Blocks arranged round core rod

Concrete filling central hole

Steel rod core hooked at ends